THE FIRST WORLD WAR 1914–18
BOOK TWO
WAR IN BRITAIN
FIONA REYNOLDSON

THE FIRST WORLD WAR 1914–18

BOOK TWO
WAR IN BRITAIN
FIONA REYNOLDSON

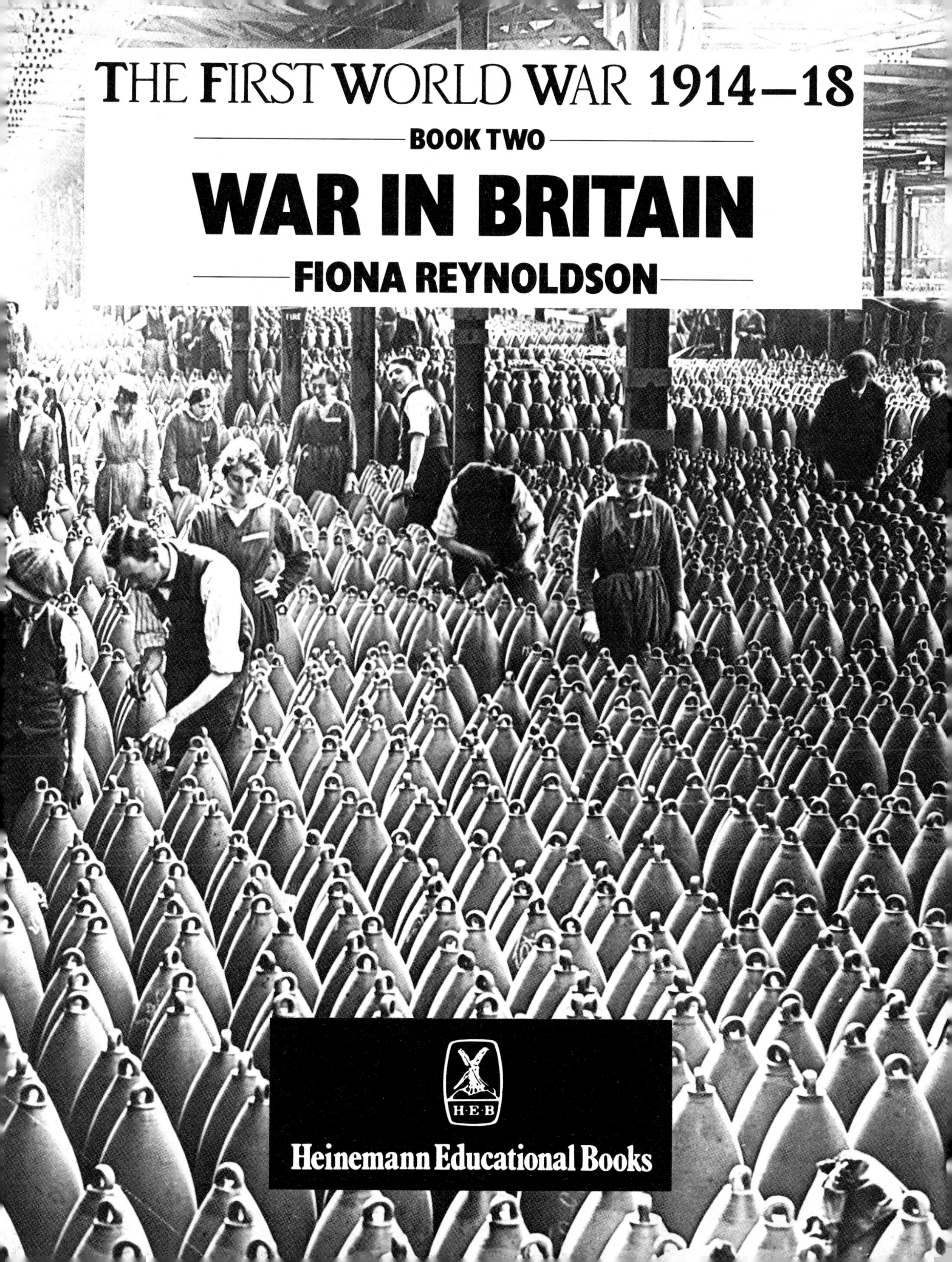

Heinemann Educational Books

Other uniform titles:

The First World War 1914–18
  Book 1 *War beyond Britain*
  by Fiona Reynoldson
Twentieth-Century British History
  Book 1 1900–14
  Book 2 1919–39
  Book 3 1945 to the 1980s
  all by Fiona Reynoldson
War at Home by Fiona Reynoldson
War in Europe by Fiona Reynoldson
War in the Far East by Fiona Reynoldson
The USA in the Twentieth Century by
  Andrew Reid
Britain's Industrial Revolution by
  Jacqueline Roberts
Ships by Clive Booth

Heinemann Educational Books Ltd
22 Bedford Square, London WC1B 3HH

LONDON EDINBURGH MELBOURNE
AUCKLAND SINGAPORE KUALA LUMPUR
NEW DELHI IBADAN NAIROBI
JOHANNESBURG PORTSMOUTH [NH]
KINGSTON

© Fiona Reynoldson 1988

First published 1988

British Library Cataloguing in Publication Data

Reynoldson, Fiona
  The First World War 1914–18
  Bk. 2: War in Britain
  1. World War, 1914–1918
  I. Title
  940.3   D522.7

ISBN 0-435-31745-8

Filmset and printed in Great Britain by
BAS Printers Limited, Over Wallop,
Hampshire

Acknowledgements

The author and publishers would like to thank the following for permission to reproduce illustrations on the pages indicated:

BBC Hulton Picture Library: pp. 1, 2, 7, 13, 16, 17, 21, 28 (top), 74 (top), 83 (lower), 84 and 85.
British Coal: p. 45.*
Trustees of the Imperial War Museum: cover; title page; pp. 25, 26 (right),† 28 (lower), 39, 43, 44, 49 (top and lower left), 50 (left and right), 53, 55 (right), 56, 57, 59, 60, 61, 65 (top), 66, 70, 71, 72, 75 (top right and lower), 76 and 83 (top).
Lady Lawson: p. 24.‡
Lincolnshire Archives Office: p. 18.
Mary Evans Picture Library: p. 8.
Popperfoto: pp. 20, 22, 47, 55 (left) and 65 (lower).
Punch Publications: pp. 5, 6, 12, 26 (left), 30, 36, 37, 38, 49 (lower right), 50 (top), 73 and 75 (top left).
Topham: pp. 9, 51 and 54.
Woman's Weekly: pp. 42, 77, 78, 79, 80, 81 and 82.
Women's International League for Peace and Freedom: pp. 33 and 34.

Artwork by Ian Foulis.

*From the collection of the late Rev. F. W. Cobb, Vicar of Eastwood.
†From PP (1919), vol. xvi, Cmnd 504.
‡From Henry Lawson, *Vignettes of the Western Front* (Positif Press, 1979).

COVER: *'Wounded men on Duppas Hill, Croydon' by Dorothy Coke.*
TITLE PAGE PHOTOGRAPH: *A munitions factory during the First World War.*

Contents

Acknowledgements   *iv*

1 **Britain Before the War**   *1*
Workers
Trade unions
Women
Ireland

2 **The Coming War**   *5*
Sarajevo
The great countries took sides
Germany's ultimatum to Belgium
2 August 1914
War fever

3 **Britain Declares War**   *8*
Bank holiday Monday, 3 August 1914
Lord Grey
War
What some people said about the war in August 1914

4 **Zeppelin Airships**   *11*
The world's first airship
Airships and aeroplanes
The first airship raid, 19 January 1915
Guns against airships
Looking for airships
24 September 1916

5 **Invasion**   *16*
Hartlepool
Invasion
Proclamation in Lincolnshire

6 **The End of Zeppelins But More Air Raids**   *20*
Effect of the zeppelins
The end of 1916
25 May 1917
More air raids
1918

7 **Recruiting**   *24*
Pals battalions
'Your Country Needs You'
Conscription
White feathers

8 **Defence of the Realm**   *28*
DORA
Dorothy Lawrence
Drink

9 **The Women's Peace Conference in the Hague, 1915**   *32*
Stop the war
Crystal Macmillan
No peace

10 **Rumours**   *36*
War
Atrocity stories
Rumours
Censorship
The problem

11 **Women in Uniform and Outside the Home**   *42*
Women's war work
Voluntary Aid Detachments
Nursing
Other women in uniform
Women's Army Auxiliary Corps

12 **To Fight or Not to Fight**   *45*
Tribunals
Conscientious objectors

13 **Propaganda**   *48*
The government
Keeping the fighting going

14 Wounded Soldiers *51*
   Walking wounded
   Regimental first aid post
   Casualty clearing station
   The seriously wounded
   The battle of the Somme, 1 July 1916

15 Munitions and Women *55*
   Woolwich Arsenal
   Women in the factories
   Conscription or exemption
   Dangerous work

16 Prisoners of War *59*
   Leonard Thompson
   German civilians in Britain
   British civilians in Germany

17 Food *63*
   Staple food
   Would Britain starve?
   The government, 1915–16
   Ministry of Food
   Rationing

18 Getting Better *70*
   Treatment
   Invalided out

19 Life at Home *73*
   Cost of the war
   Government control
   Other government control
   Food control
   Jobs to be done
   Training camps
   Bombing

20 A Woman's Magazine *77*

21 The End of the War *83*
   Vera Brittain
   Survivors
   War memorials
   The future
   The unknown warrior

Index *86*

1 Britain Before the War

Britain was torn by troubles before the war. It seemed as though law and order were about to break down. In particular, three groups of people were discontented: many of the working class, some women and most of the Irish.

Workers

In the nineteenth century Britain was the richest country in the world. Its industries were very successful. It made huge fortunes by exporting goods all over the world. Britain had the biggest empire ever seen. It had the most powerful navy.

But by the start of the twentieth century Britain was falling behind. Other nations were struggling to get empires. Countries like Germany and the USA now had modern industries. They were starting to take customers away from Britain. To make matters worse, Germany was building a big navy which could one day be better than Britain's navy.

All this meant that Britain had to make goods more cheaply if it was going to be able to sell them abroad. It also meant that Britain had to spend lots of money on new ships for the navy.

The easiest way to make goods more cheaply was to pay workers low wages and make them work long hours. Many women and men worked very long hours. They earned very little money. They were unhappy. Some looked to trade unions to help them.

Leonard Thompson left school when he was 13. At first he worked in the fields harvesting beets. He was paid 2s 6d (12½p) for working 60 hours a week.

A ship full of emigrants leaving Tilbury dock in 1912.

2 The First World War 1914–18

> ### Source 1.1
> 'Then I went to work for a farmer driving cattle and sheep to Ipswich market. I got 4s 6d [22½p] a week and I walked 25 miles a day. Then I got into a row. I'd driven a flock of sheep from Ipswich and the next morning they found that one had died. The farmer ran down the field and met my mother on her way to chapel. I had driven the sheep too hard, he said. 'And you drive boys too hard!' she said – she had no fear at all. Well the truth of the matter is that she said a lot of things she'd only thought until then, and so I left the farm. It must seem that there there was war between farmers and their men in those days. I think there was, particularly in Suffolk. They took all they could from the men and boys who worked their land. They bought their life's strength for as little as they could. They wore us out without a thought because, with big families, there was a continuous supply of labour.'
>
> From Ronald Blythe, *Akenfield* (Allen Lane, 1969).

Trade unions

Some workers joined trade unions. The trade unions wanted workers to earn more money. They wanted them to work shorter hours. They wanted better conditions. The only weapon that workers had against employers was the strike. In the years before 1914 there were many strikes.

Strikes

The dockers went on strike in 1911. The transport workers went on strike in 1912. Some of these strikes led to street fighting. The police, and even the army, had to be called in to control them. Some workers even talked about revolution.

Meat vans leaving the docks for Smithfield Market in London during the transport strike of May 1912.

Women

Poor women worked hard. Many had miserable lives.

> ### Source 1.2
> 'When he was out of work she often pretended, as she gave him his meals, that she had had hers while he was out. And all this time the baby was draining her life away and her work was never done.'
>
> From Robert Tressell, *The Ragged Trousered Philanthropists* (Granada, 1965).

Rich women often did not have enough to do. Many hated the useless lives that they led. Vera Brittain longed to go to university. It was so easy for her brother to go to university. It was nearly impossible for a girl.

Suffragettes and suffragists

Many women wanted a better life. They wanted more rights. Suffragettes and suffragists wanted women to have the right to vote. This means the right to vote for the people who make laws in Parliament.

Suffragettes often acted violently. They wanted people to notice them. Then people would listen. **Suffragists** thought that violence was wrong. They felt people would listen if women argued quietly and sensibly, but they too said that women must have the vote. This would be the beginning of fair treatment for women.

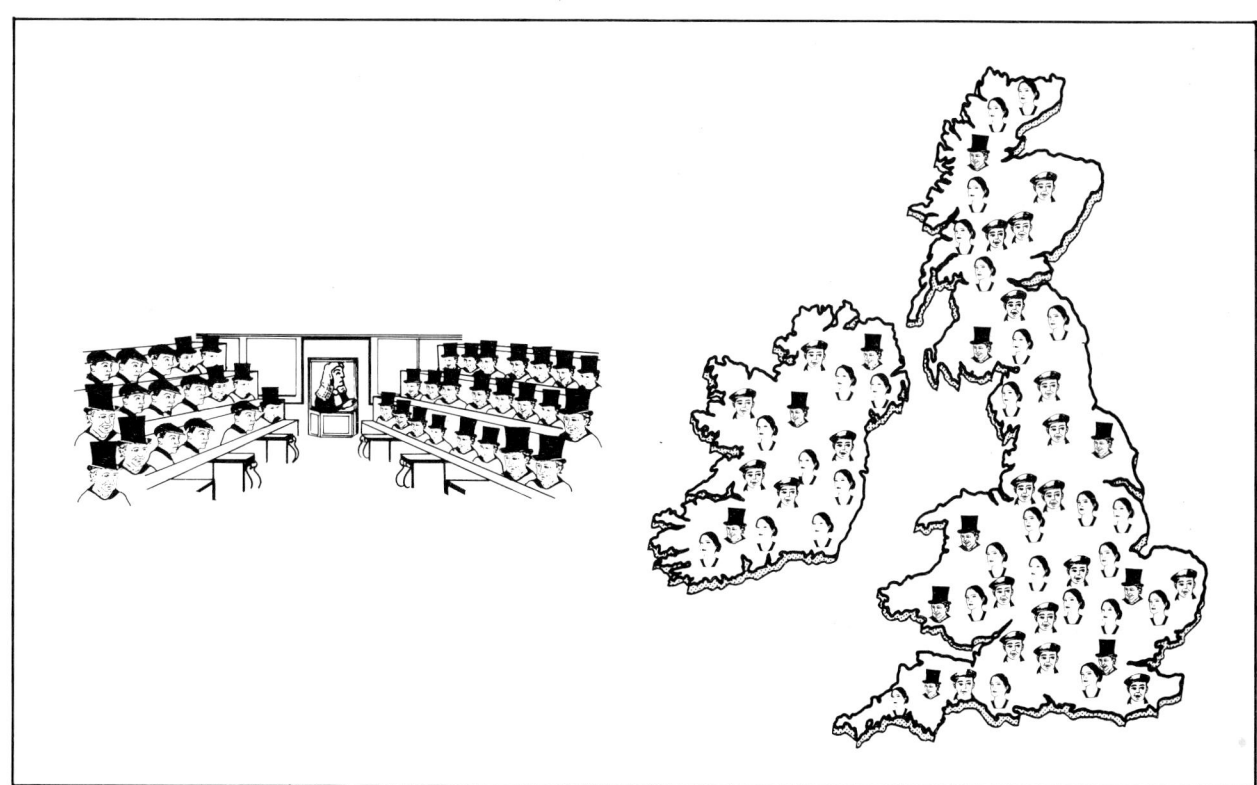

Half the people in Britain were women. All women and men had to obey the laws. Laws were made in Parliament. But only men sat in Parliament. The Members of Parliament were elected by men.

Ireland

The whole of Ireland was still part of Britain in 1914. Catholics made up a large part of the population of Ireland. Some people in Britain wanted home rule for Ireland. (That meant Ireland could make its own rules for home affairs.) Many people in northern Ireland hated the idea of home rule. They felt very British. They wanted to stay as part of Britain. Many of these people were Protestants.

Nearly civil war

Sir Edward Carson led the Protestants in northern Ireland. He set up an army of 80,000 men. At once, the southern Irish set up an army. Both sides were ready to fight. The British government decided to step in. The British Government was ready to send the British army to try to keep the peace. But the government soon found that it could not trust the army. Many British officers in Ireland said they would leave the army. They were Protestants. They would not fight other Protestants in northern Ireland.

Both the Irish armies started to smuggle guns. Nobody could agree about Ireland and home rule. In July 1914 it looked as if civil war was about to break out in Britain.

So there was a lot to worry about by the year 1914. Britain was a troubled country. Then suddenly things changed. It looked as if war was going to break out in Europe.

Things to Do

1 Which three groups of people in Britain were discontented before the war (lines 4–6)?

2 Which other two countries had modern industries by the start of the twentieth century (lines 16–17)?
3 In what other way did one of these countries rival Britain (lines 20–22)?
4 What did Britain do to try to keep ahead of its rivals (lines 23–7)?
5 What was home rule for Ireland (lines 105–6)?
6 Who hated home rule? Why do you think they hated it?
7 The British government was horrified by the threat of British officers to leave the army. Why do you think it was so worried? Do you think soldiers should be free to decide who they should fight? Talk about this in class.
8 Read Source 1.1.
   (a) What reason is given for farmers paying low wages for long hours?
   (b) Were all working people frightened of their employers?
   (c) How would it have helped if Leonard had joined a trade union?
   (d) What difficulties would farm workers in Suffolk have come across if they had tried to set up a trade union at that time?
9 Read Source 1.2.
   (a) Do you think that the woman was fond of her husband? Give a reason for your answer.
   (b) Why was being poor often worse for a woman than a man?
10 Source 1.3 is from Mrs Pankhurst's speech in the dock at Bow Street Court in 1908. Mrs Pankhurst was a leading suffragette. She had been arrested for trying to force her way into the House of Commons.

> **Source 1.3**
>
> 'We have tried every way. We have presented petitions. We have held great public meetings. For this we have been ridiculed.
> Now, sir, I say to you that I come here not as an ordinary law breaker. I should never be here if I had the same kind of laws that the very meanest and commonest of men have – the same power to vote that the wife beater has, the same power that the drunkard has. This is the only way we can get that power which everyone should have of deciding how the taxes women, as well as men, pay should be made. Until we get that power we shall be here again and again. We are going to win. Well sir, that is all I have to say to you. We are here not because we are law breakers. We are here in our efforts to become law makers.'
>
> From Leslie Baily, *BBC Scrapbook 1900–14* (Frederick Muller, 1957).

   (a) Why was Mrs Pankhurst in court? What sort of offence do you think she was charged with?
   (b) What was her aim?
   (c) Explain why she had committed the offence.
   (d) Do you think her attitude was right? How would you go about getting the vote?
   (e) What were the differences between the lives of the two women in Sources 1.2 and 1.3?
   (f) What are the differences between the lives of women you know and the lives of those in Sources 1.2 and 1.3?

2 The Coming War

By about 1900 the great countries of Europe were afraid of each other. They all looked for friends. They signed treaties. They became allies. They were all armed to the teeth. They expected a war. There were two main groups of allies:

The Triple Alliance	**The Triple Entente**
Germany	France
Austria	Russia
Italy	Britain

Sarajevo

It was 28 June 1914. Far away from Britain the Archduke Franz Ferdinand was shot in Sarajevo by a Serbian. The Archduke was the heir to the Austrian throne. Austria was furious. Austria blamed Serbia for the Archduke's death.

What followed was like a whirlpool. The great countries of Europe jumped into the whirlpool. It was a whirlpool to war.

The great countries took sides

Germany stood up for Austria. Russia stood up for Serbia. France stood up for Russia. Everyone in Europe was on edge. War was very close.

Germany decided to attack France. On 2 August 1914 Germany was ready to march through Belgium to invade France. Now Britain was furious. Britain said that Germany and Britain and other countries had signed an agreement in 1839. The agreement said that Belgium was to be a neutral country. This meant that no other country was to invade Belgium. Now Germany was ready to invade Belgium. This was the last straw. Britain felt it must help Belgium. The British government had given its word in 1839.

THE POWER BEHIND.

This cartoon appeared in July 1914. The animal symbol of Russia is a bear. What is the symbol of Austria? How does the artist make you think that Serbia (Servia) is unimportant? Between which sides is the war going to be fought?

Germany's ultimatum to Belgium

The Kaiser of Germany sent an ultimatum to the king of Belgium. The
40 kaiser said that Belgium could stay a free country but Belgium must let German soldiers march through Belgium. Belgium said no. So German soldiers fought their way into Belgium.

BRAVO, BELGIUM!

Choose the words from the brackets that you think best describe what is happening in this cartoon which appeared in August 1914:

1 *(Britain/Germany/France) wants to invade Belgium.*
2 *'No Thoroughfare' means (free parking/you can't go this way).*
3 *The artist sees Germany as (a bully/greedy/friendly/big/reasonable).*
4 *The artist sees Belgium as (foolish/small/brave/wise).*

'Crowds cheering at the declaration of war, Trafalgar Square, London 1914.'
  This is the caption on the back of the photograph which comes from a photo library. Look carefully.

1 *Is everyone in the crowd cheering?*
2 *Where are most 'cheerers'?*
3 *In whose direction are many of them looking?*
4 *How do you know that they are cheering?*
5 *How is the woman in the centre showing that she is cheering?*
6 *Does this photograph prove that most people wanted war? What other evidence would you want to have to convince yourself that war was welcomed enthusiastically by most people?*

2 August 1914

45 It was Sunday 2 August 1914. In Britain thousands of people were on holiday. It was a bank holiday weekend. They were very excited. They were very worried. What was going to happen? Was there
50 going to be a war?
  Thousands of people gathered outside Buckingham Palace. They cheered. They heard that the British navy had mobilized for war. They cheered again. They sang
55 'God Save the King'. Surely Britain would go to war now? Britain must join France and Russia against Germany and Austria. All Europe would be at war.

War fever

People forgot Ireland. They forgot the
60 suffragettes. They forgot strikes and trade unions. Britain was great. Britain was going to war. Britain was right to fight for Belgium. It was exciting.
  German people thought they were
65 right. Germany was great. War was exciting. It was the same all over Europe.
  A few people were not so sure. One of these people was the American ambassador in Britain.

Source 2.1

'So the Grand Smash is come. I walked out into the night a while ago. Stars are bright, the country quiet as peace itself. Millions of men are in army camps and on war ships. Will they have to fight and many of them die – to untangle this network of treaties and alliances with gunpowder so that the world may start again?'

'The Life and Letters of Walter H. Page'. From G. Marcus, *Before the Lamps Went Out* (George Allen & Unwin, 1965).

Things to Do

1. Which countries belonged to the Triple Alliance (lines 7–10)?
2. Which countries belonged to the Triple Entente (lines 7–10)?
3. Read the section headed '2 August 1914'. What did the British crowds want?
4. What evidence is there that the British looked to the king to give a lead?
5. Do you think most British people approved of the feelings shown in the photograph above?
6. Look at a map of Europe. Why do you think Britain did not want a strong, great country controlling Belgium?
7. Read Source 2.1.
    (a) Why was Walter Page not caught up in the war fever?
    (b) What tells you that he had been expecting a major war?
    (c) What else tells you in the chapter (illustrations or text) that a major war was expected by many at some time.

3 Britain Declares War

Bank holiday Monday, 3 August 1914

The sun shone on and off all day. Thousands of people went to the zoo. 17,000 people watched Surrey play Nottinghamshire at the Oval Cricket Ground in London. Thousands went to fairgrounds and to the seaside. They enjoyed themselves. But war was not far away.

Children were excited. They saw train loads of soldiers and sailors. The trains steamed slowly out of the big London stations.

Source 3.1

'Newsboys shouted out the headlines on every street corner.

"Invasion of France, Germany's ultimatum to Belgium, England and the war!"'

From G. Marcus, *Before the Lamps Went Out* (George Allen & Unwin, 1965).

Bank holiday at Ramsgate.

Lord Grey

Lord Grey was Britain's foreign secretary. He made a speech in the House of Commons. He said that Britain must stand by France and help Belgium. The members of the House of Commons shouted and cheered. Only a few were against the war.

> *Source 3.2*
>
> ' Lord Grey left the House of Commons with Winston Churchill. Churchill said:
> "What happens now?"
> "Now," said Lord Grey, "We shall send an ultimatum to Germany. They must stop invading Belgium within 24 hours." '
>
> From G. Marcus, *Before the Lamps Went Out* (George Allen & Unwin, 1965).

War

Britain sent the ultimatum but Germany carried on marching through Belgium. It was 4 August 1914.

What some people said about the war in August 1914

> *Source 3.3*
> **4 August 1914**
>
> ' Baby went for her first summer holiday to Llandudno for four weeks. She had great fun on the sands with a bucket and spade and also had donkey rides on Jasper. War was declared between England and Germany on Monday August 4 1914. '
>
> From the unpublished diary of Mrs S. Lloyd.

> *Source 3.4*
> **August**
>
> ' Lord Kitchener was put in charge of the army. The government asked him how many soldiers he needed. He said the war would last three years. He would need at least one million men. The government was astonished. '
>
> From Dennis Winter, *Death's Men: Soldiers of the Great War* (Allen Lane, 1978).

A lamplighter trimming a gas lamp. The gas lamps had to be lit every evening. When war was declared Lord Grey looked into the street, where a lamplighter was climbing a ladder, and said to his friend: 'The lamps of Europe are going out one by one.'

> *Source 3.5*
> **4 August**
>
> ' Now that the war is here "it will be in the kitchen that the pinch will be felt". '
>
> From the *Bradford Daily Argus*.

> *Source 3.6*
> **14 August**
>
> ' What with the war and the rain, last Saturday was a most depressing day for the Catford Cricket Club. '
>
> From the *Catford Journal*.

Source 3.7
11 August

'The music school of the German town of Dresden advertised its new courses in music. They would start on 1 April 1915. The advertisement said that they expected a "speedy return to normal".'

From the *Swindon Advertiser*.

Things to Do

1 What was the most important news for Mrs Lloyd (lines 34–9)?
2 How many men did Lord Kitchener say he would need (lines 44–5)?
3 How long did Kitchener say the war would last (lines 43–4)?
4 Which word best describes how the government felt about what Lord Kitchener said?

   annoyed   surprised
   relieved astounded

5 Choose the people from the following list that would be worst affected by the war, according to the *Bradford Daily Argus*:

   chefs   soldiers   miners
   policemen housewives   sailors
   nurses   telephonists cooks
   farmers   millers   tinplate workers

Which people do **you** think would be worst affected by the war?

6 Look at Source 3.7. What do you think 'a speedy return to normal' means?
7 Look at Sources 3.3–3.7 in class. Which of the writers thought the war was not all that important?
8 Which source shows that the writer thought the war would be short?
9 Which source shows that one person thought the war would be long and serious? Did the government agree with him?

4 Zeppelin Airships

The world's first airship

In 1900 Count von Zeppelin built an airship. It was over 100 metres long. (A classroom is about ten metres long.) It looked like a giant, cigar-shaped balloon.

Airships and aeroplanes

Airships, balloons and aeroplanes fascinated people. Maybe at last people could fly. In 1903 the Wright Brothers built an aeroplane. It flew for a few seconds. It was the beginning of a dream come true. But it could be a nightmare too.

Airships and aeroplanes can fly high above towns. They can fly high above soldiers and ships. (Think of at least two ways in which airships and aeroplanes can be used in war.)

A zeppelin of 1916.

Length: *196.9 metres*
Cruising range: *2,300 miles*
Engines: *6 × 240 h.p. engines*
Crew: *22 men*

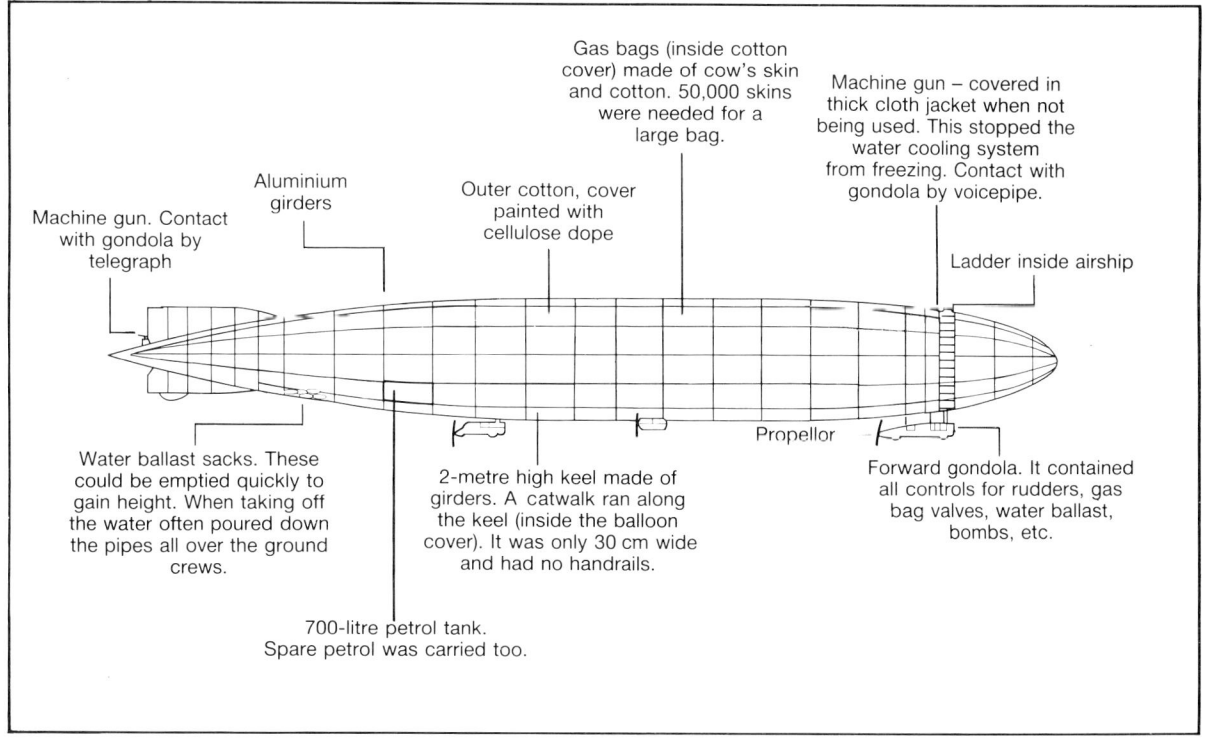

The first airship raid, 19 January 1915

Kaiser Wilhelm was the king of Germany. He was worried. He did not want to bomb British homes. He said the zeppelin airships must only bomb special targets.

Three giant zeppelins left Germany. The moon was nearly full and bright over the dark North Sea. The weather was fine at first. Then the rain started. Soon there were snow showers as well. It was impossible to see. One of the airships had engine trouble. It went back to Germany.

Two of the airships reached Britain. But they did not know where they were. Captain Fritz's airship was L3. The rainwater on the huge balloon was very heavy. It pressed the airship down. It flew lower and lower. At 1,520 metres Captain Fritz threw out a parachute flare. It lit up the ground below. It helped him to guess where he was. He was over Great Yarmouth. He dropped bombs for ten minutes. Then he turned his great silver balloon for home.

'Cyclist to policeman: "Douse your glim, mate; we'll be having them Zeppelins all over us."' What is the cyclist worried about? (This cartoon appeared in October 1914.)

The zeppelins were to bomb the London docks and places where guns and bombs were made. They also were to bomb the naval dockyards and oil storage tanks along the River Thames.

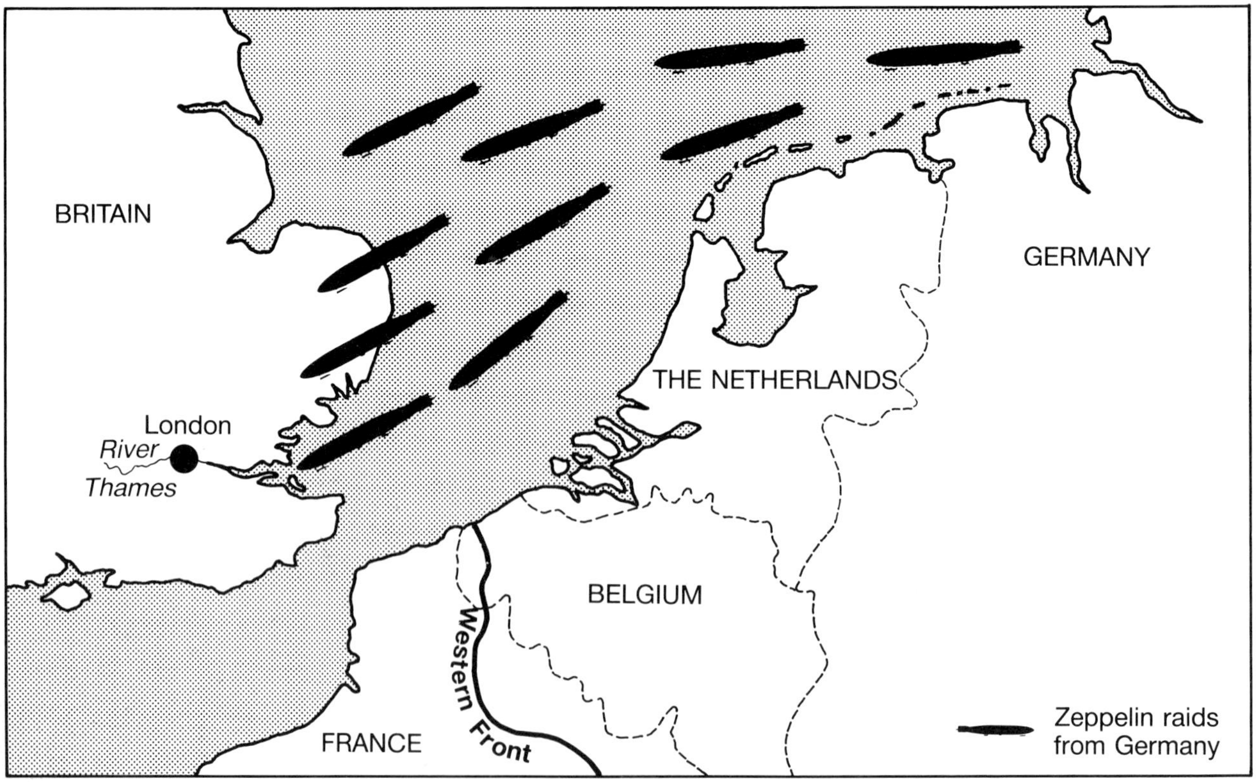

Great Yarmouth

The bombs killed two people. The bombs hit many houses. The other airship bombed King's Lynn. But people were not very scared. They were puzzled. Where were the British planes? Where were the British guns? Why had they not shot down the zeppelin airships?

Guns against airships

The aeroplanes had not taken off in time. There were very few guns in Britain for shooting airships. The guns could not fire high enough in the air. Soon factories made more big guns. Factories made more aeroplanes. They made more search lights. The search lights lit up the airships in the sky. Then the guns shot at the airships.

Looking for airships

It was not very easy to find the airships. Source 4.1 shows how difficult it was.

The LZ95 was finally shot down after a bombing raid in France in 1916.

> *Source 4.1*
> **3 September 1916**
>
> 'The night was very dark and in the early evening dense with low clouds [300 metres] and fine rain; later the sky cleared leaving gaps in the clouds. We could see airships between clouds and through thin cloud up to 6,000 yards [5,800 metres]. As soon as the search light was switched on it could follow the airship only in the gaps. Even through thin cloud the glare of the search light made the airship invisible as in a fog.
> We noticed that the airships are very clever at keeping behind cloud.'
>
> A. Rawlinson, Commanding RNAA Mobile Brigade. From A. Rawlinson, *The Defence of London 1915–18* (Andrew Melrose, 1923).

24 September 1916

The zeppelin airships kept coming. Twelve of these great airships set out from Germany. Captain Böcker flew the L33. He reached London. The British guns were firing. Böcker kept on. He was not hit. He wanted the airship to fly higher. So he dropped water ballast. His airship lifted to 4,000 metres over London. It was 11 pm. He let go his bombs.

The bombing

80 Houses, timber yards and oil barrels burst into flames below him. He turned for home. He was still safe. Then a shell burst into the balloon. It shredded five gas bags. It made holes in even more. Hydrogen
85 hissed out into the freezing air. It was amazing that the airship did not catch fire.

The airship dives to the ground

The airship dived at 250 metres a minute. The German crew climbed high in the
90 balloon. Their hands froze. They tried to mend the gas bags. The British guns kept firing. A British plane found the airship among the clouds.

> *Source 4.2*
>
> 'The ammunition seemed to be bursting all
95 along it, but the zepp did not catch fire. I decided to get above the zepp and went on climbing but lost it completely in a bank of grey cloud.'
>
> Lieutenant A. de Brandon. From R. L. Rimell, *Zeppelin!* (Conway, 1984).

The airship was doomed. The crew
100 threw out everything to lighten the airship. But it hit the ground in a field in Essex.

The crash

The crew of twenty-one men were all right. Captain Böcker banged on the
105 doors of cottages nearby. He shouted for people to come out. He was going to set fire to the airship. It might blow up. It did not. So the British found out a great deal about German airships.

The arrest of the crew of L33

110 Captain Böcker called his men to attention. They set off down the lane. The huge glow of the burning zeppelin lit the hedgerows as the men marched in the dark. They came round a corner. Special
115 Constable Edgar Nicholas was cycling towards them. He turned on his torch. It lit the faces of the tired Germans. They spent the rest of the war as prisoners.

Things to Do

1 Who was Kaiser Wilhelm (line 17)?
2 Why do you think he did not want to bomb British homes?
3 What did he want the zeppelins to bomb (lines 19–20)?
4 What sort of places would the kaiser think were special targets?
5 Read through the section headed 'Guns against airships'. Then answer the questions in the section headed 'Great Yarmouth'.
6 Read Source 4.1.
   (a) What problems did the searchlight teams have in tracking airships?
   (b) What was the date of A. Rawlinson's report?
   (c) What tells you that this report was in the early days of air warfare?
7 Read Source 4.2.
   (a) What problems did the zeppelin crews, the aeroplane crews and the searchlight teams all face, according to this source?
   (b) Where else in the chapter are these problems mentioned?
8 What other problems did the crews of airships and aeroplanes face in the early days of flying? How have these problems been overcome today?
9 What do you think were the reactions of Special Constable Edgar Nicholas and the German airship crew when they met? What choices did the Germans have? Make up a conversation between

the constable and the captain. The German captain spoke good English. He would have spoken for his men. The constable spoke no German. He was alone.

10 Do the crossword. (*Numbers in brackets after some clues refer to text line numbers. You will need to read the whole sentence to find the answer.*)

ACROSS

1 So he dropped water ————. (77)
6 He did ——— want to bomb British homes. (18)
7 He was going to set ———— to the airship. (106)
8 —— the British found out a great deal about German airships. (108)
11 Short for Wireless Telegraphy.
13 He turned on ——— torch. (116)
14 Hydrogen hissed ——— into the freezing air. (84)
16 Count von ———————— built an airship. (1)
19 'We noticed that the airships are very clever at keeping —————— cloud.' (69)
20 Even through thin cloud the glare of the search light made the airship invisible as in a ———. (66)

DOWN

2 The crew threw out everything to lighten the ————————. (99)
3 Captain Fritz's airship was ——. (30)
4 Soon there were ———— showers as well. (24)
5 It helped him —— guess where he was. (35)
7 Captain —————— airship was L3. (30)
9 It was amazing that the airship did not ————— fire. (85)
10 The huge glow of the burning zeppelin lit the hedgerows —— the men marched in the dark. (111)
12 Airships and aeroplanes can fly high above —————. (12)
15 'I decided to get above the zepp and went on climbing but lost it completely in a bank of grey —————.' (95)
17 —— was going to set fire to the airship. (106)
18 His airship lifted —— 4,000 metres over London. (77)

5 Invasion

Hartlepool

German ships sailed close to Hartlepool. On 16 December 1914 the ships shelled Hartlepool. 119 people, including babies and children, were killed. People were
5 terrified and angry. They were afraid that Germany was going to invade Britain. They also hated the Germans for shelling the town. They would not give in.

Scarborough and Whitby were also
10 shelled.

Invasion

Perhaps the Germans really would invade. What should ordinary people do if the Germans invaded?

A shop wrecked by shells in the German bombardment of Scarborough in December 1914. What differences can you see between this street scene and a street scene today?

Source 5.1
Monday 18 January 1915: meeting of special constables, Great Leighs, Essex

'The chairman, Major William Brown, said that an emergency committee had for some weeks been in session. There was to be a similar committee in every police division of the county to assume direction of people and cattle in case of enemy landing. The special constables in each parish would have the duty of directing the people along the route chosen.'

From Reverend A. Clark, *Echoes of the Great War* (OUP, 1985).

Proclamation in Lincolnshire

A proclamation was sent out in Lincolnshire (see Source 5.2 on page 18). It was sent to military commanders on the east coast. They kept the proclamation secret. It was only to be shown to ordinary people if the Germans really invaded. A few months later it was obvious the Germans were not going to invade Britain. So all the proclamations were handed in.

Special constables.

The east coast of England. Look at a map of Europe in an atlas to see which counties were most likely to be attacked by Germany.

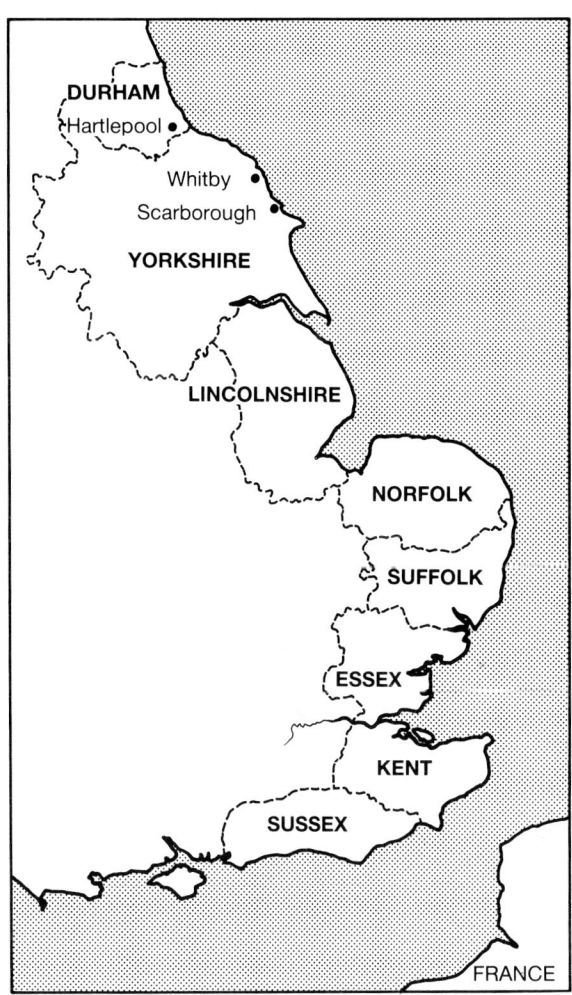

Source 5.2

PROCLAMATION

DEFENCE OF THE REALM.

THE ENEMY HAVING INVADED THIS COAST

The Civil population are hereby directed to carry out the following instructions:—

1. Under the arrangements made, all motors, bicycles, horses, mules, donkeys, carts, carriages, and other vehicles, harness, petrol, launches, and lighters, must be forthwith moved to the place arranged. If these objects cannot be immediately moved, they must be destroyed or rendered useless.

2. Failing other orders from the Military Authorities, live stock will be driven into fields off the road and scattered as much as possible.

3. **NO ATTEMPT**, except under orders from the Military Authorities or the Police acting under such orders, should be made to burn, cut or destroy:—

   Bridges
   Railway Rolling Stock
   Electric Light or Power Stations
   Telegraph or Telephone Wires
   Wireless Stations
   Waterworks
   Sluices or Locks
   Piers or Jetties
   Ferries

   The arrangements already made with the Police should be carried out.

4. All tools, pick-axes, spades, shovels, felling-axes, saws, barbed wire and other equipment must be taken to the place appointed.

5. <u>**Keep the roads clear for the Military**</u>. Free passage for all troops must be preserved. This is most important, and to neglect it will hamper and obstruct the Military Forces proceeding to defend the shore and will be dangerous to the obstructors.

6. Prompt assistance should be given to the Military Authorities if and when required for any purpose whatsoever.

7. No Civil Inhabitants should under any circumstances use firearms against the invading forces of the enemy. Anyone disregarding this Instruction will possibly endanger the lives and property of his defenceless neighbours.

8. Paragraph 7 does not apply to men who are enrolled in the National Volunteer Corps as officially recognised by the War Office, who will have the rights of belligerents.

By Order,

EARL BROWNLOW,

Lord Lieutenant of Lincolnshire.

A. WATERHOUSE, MONSON ST., LINCOLN.

Things to Do

1 Fill in the gaps. (*Numbers in brackets refer to text line numbers.*)

German ----- (1) sailed close to Hartlepool. It was 16 -------- (2) 1914. The ships ------- (2) Hartlepool. 119 people, including ------ (3) and children, were killed.

2 Read Source 5.1.

  (a) In which county were emergency committees set up?
  (b) Who was the enemy?
  (c) Who was to direct people and cattle if the enemy landed?
  (d) Which animals, apart from cattle, do you think the enemy would want to make use of in 1915?
  (e) When do you think the first emergency committee was set up?

3 Look at Source 5.2.
  (a) Who ordered the proclamation to be issued? What was his job?
  (b) Why do you think 'all motors, bicycles . . .' must be moved to the place arranged or destroyed?
  (c) What do you think livestock is? What is to happen to the livestock? Is this the same as the directions for livestock in Essex?

  (d) Read number 3 in the proclamation carefully. Look at the list. If you were the invading Germans, which do you think would be the most important things to capture? Write out the list in the order you think is most important. If you think waterworks are the most important, write that first. Talk about your choices in class.
  (e) Imagine that you are living in Hartlepool in 1915. The Germans have invaded Britain. There are German soldiers knocking at the door of your house. How would you speak to them? How would they behave? What do you think they might ask you? What does the proclamation tell you to do if you meet invading Germans? Why do you think this is? What would you do?

7 Imagine it is 1915. The enemy is invading from the sea and coming towards *your* town, city or nearest town. You are in charge of all movements on the roads. You have been told to delay the enemy as long as possible. Work out your orders for soldiers, sailors, children, farmers, bus drivers, telephone workers, gas workers, electricity workers, old people, mothers or fathers with babies, railway engine drivers, shop workers and so on. You need to know the roads and other routes around your town. What problems do you think you will have?

◀ *This proclamation was kept secret. Twenty copies were issued to local military commanders. When the invasion scare was over the twenty copies were called back in to be destroyed. By mistake an extra copy had clung to the back of the twentieth copy. The person handed in the twentieth copy and kept the twenty-first copy! This is it. Why do you think the proclamation was kept secret from ordinary people?*

6 The End of Zeppelins But More Air Raids

The zeppelin raids on Britain did not work. They did not destroy aircraft factories, ships and docks or huge oil storage tanks. It was impossible to aim the bombs accurately. Often the zeppelin crews did not even know where they were.

All the time Britain was building bigger guns and better aeroplanes. Soon the aeroplanes could climb high and fast. They could climb above the zeppelins. Then the zeppelins could be easily shot down.

Effect of the zeppelins

The zeppelin airships came like great, beautiful silver balloons. People rushed into the streets to see them in the moonlight or in the search lights. But then they dropped bombs. Houses burnt. People were killed. This was the first time that death came from the sky. Britain was not a safe island any more.

Many people were terrified. Mr and Mrs Lockyer had two small daughters. They decided to leave south London. They sold their dairy. They moved to Buckinghamshire. They felt safe from zeppelins there.

The end of 1916

Then nothing happened for six months. Maybe it was all over. Maybe Britain could not be bombed from the air. But the real danger was from aeroplanes.

25 May 1917

Twenty-three German bombers flew over Folkestone. People shopping looked up.

A German bomber, 1915. Find the new 'special apparatus' for bomb dropping.

This was how bombs were dropped at first. This is a Russian armoured plane. The officer is fixing the bomb on the side before starting. Soon the Germans began to develop a bombsight. The 'bomber' sat in front of the pilot. He looked down a long tube fitted with lenses and prisms. He had to work out the height and speed of the aeroplane. Then he could use the bombsight to know when to drop the bomb so it would (possibly!) hit the target. However, accurate bombing remained very difficult.

Source 6.1

' I heard them before I saw them. I guessed at once they were German. We didn't have anything which made that kind of noise. It was a throbbing hum. '

Captain C. Russell,
RFC pilot on leave from France.
From H.G.Castle, *Fire Over England*
(Secker & Warburg, 1982).

Suddenly there were shattering bangs. The bombs hit the harbour. But they also hit the main shopping street. It was narrow and crowded.

Source 6.2

' The whole street seemed to explode. There were smoke and flames all over, but the worst of all were the screams of the wounded and dying and mothers looking frantically for their kids. '

Canadian Sergeant Major
on leave from France.

A greengrocer's shop was bombed. Everyone inside was killed. Many people were queueing outside. They were killed or injured.

The raid lasted ten minutes. Ninety-five people were killed and 195 injured.

More air raids

Bombs fell thick and fast in many places. Siegfried Sassoon went to Liverpool Street Station. He wanted to catch the train to Cambridge. He heard bangs and crashes. He heard screams and cries. Three or four bombs hit the station. Suddenly there was no 12 o'clock train any more. Sassoon stared, stunned.

22 *The First World War 1914–18*

Source 6.3

60 ⟨ I stood wondering what to do. A luggage trolley trundled past me; on it lay an elderly man shabbily dressed and dead. And my train was not going to start. ⟩

From Siegfried Sassoon, *Memoirs of an Infantry Officer* (Faber & Faber, 1930).

Offices, shops, houses, schools –
65 nowhere was safe. The German bombers flew high. They flew at over 4,000 metres. The British guns could not reach them.

Source 6.4

⟨ They might just as well have been using pea-shooters. ⟩

Wireless telegraphist, Dover Patrol.

◀ *Air raid warning, 1917. Find out what system was used for air raid warning in the Second World War.*

British and German airbases. Germany occupied Belgium. German bombers flew from airbases in Belgium.

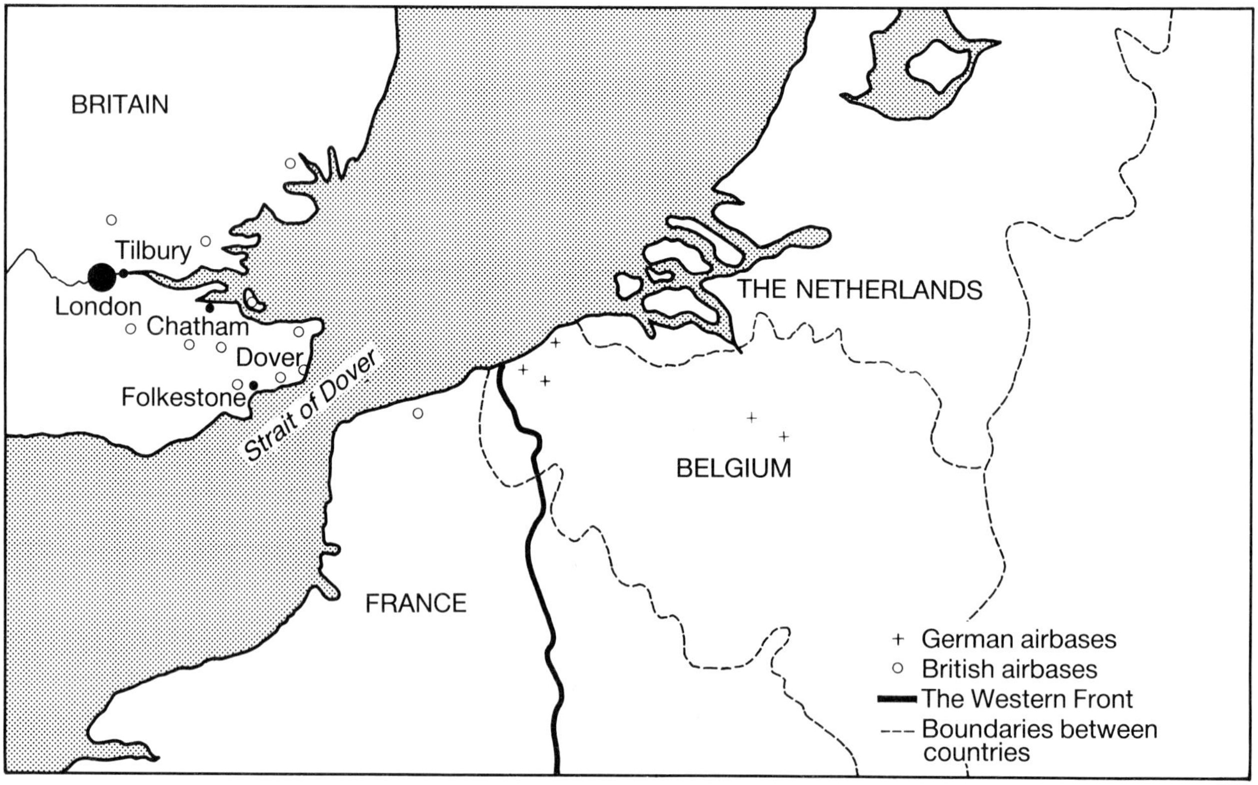

+ German airbases
○ British airbases
━ The Western Front
--- Boundaries between countries

1918

The war ended in November. 1,400 people had been killed in air raids. Over 3,000 had been injured. Far more people were killed and injured in the Second World War in air raids. But the First World War was the first time Britain was bombed. It was a terrible shock.

Things to Do

1 Which flying machine was developed most quickly during the war – the airship or the aeroplane (lines 7–10)?
2 Read the section headed 'Effect of the zeppelins'. How did the British people feel about the zeppelins?
3 How many people were killed in air raids in Britain in the First World War (lines 70–71)?
4 Imagine you were a shopper in Folkestone on 25 May 1917. You are queueing at the greengrocers. Describe what you see and hear. Below are some words to help you:

throbbing hum	running
bangs	smashed
screams	crashed
crowded	cabbages
potatoes	glass
blood	terror

You could make this into a diary entry or a letter to a friend.

5 Design a poster to warn people about air raids. Use the information and illustrations in Chapters 4 and 6 to help.

7 Recruiting

'I shall need one million men,' Lord Kitchener told the government.

And he got them. Men rushed to join the army. They thought the war would be short. They did not want to miss out.

> *Source 7.1*
>
> 'I had a dead end job in a dead end town. Here was a chance to see the world, and boys like me hadn't the money to travel then.'
>
> Alfred Blake, personal memories.

> *Source 7.2*
>
> 'I feel I am meant to take an active part in this war. It is to me a very fascinating thing – something if often horrible, yet very ennobling and very beautiful.'
>
> Roland Leighton. From Vera Brittain, *Testament of Youth* (Victor Gollancz, 1933).

> *Source 7.3*
>
> 'Mac came down to the workshop that morning.
> "I'm joining," he said, "Are you?"
> "All right," I said, "But don't tell my Mum."
> I was just 19 years old.'
>
> John Sanderson, personal memories.

They were among thousands of others. Some were older, some were under 18 and lied about their age.

> *Source 7.4*
>
> '"Eighteen, by Jove!" said the Colonel. "You've timed your lives wonderfully my boys. Nowadays you boys are the richest thing England has got."'
>
> From E. Raymond, *Tell England* (Cassell, 1922).

Henry Lawson was shortsighted, but he was determined to join the army. While he had his medical examination, he kept on his glasses and memorized the letters on the board. He was then able to read them out from memory when his eyes were tested.

Pals battalions

Friends joined up together. Often they formed pals battalions. A battalion was about 1,000 men. Footballers joined together. Artists joined together. Friends from the same town joined together. Whole football teams joined together and so on.

The advertisement in Source 7.5 appeared in a newspaper in September 1914.

> *Source 7.5*
>
> '"West End men wanted for a Pals Battalion." Shop assistants, drapers, window dressers – they could all join the army together.'
>
> From E. S. Turner, *Dear Old Blighty* (Michael Joseph, 1980).

This meant that friends stayed together. But it also meant that friends were killed together. At the battle of the Somme in 1916 many pals battalions were almost wiped out. So whole towns lost nearly all their young men.

'Your Country Needs You'

Kitchener needed more and more soldiers. So hundreds of posters were made. Leaflets and books were written to get men to join the army.

Source 7.6
❛From the very hour in which Germany forced war upon this country, the question: "How can I help?" began to be asked.❜

From A. J. Dawson, *How to Help Lord Kitchener* (Hodder & Stoughton, 1914).

CONDITIONS OF SERVICE.

If you wish to join *for the duration of the War* you must be medically fit, and satisfy the following conditions:—

Height ... 5 feet 3 inches and upwards.
Chest ... At least 34 inches.
Age ... 19 to 35, except for ex-soldiers, who will be accepted up to 45 and certain selected ex-N.C.Os. up to 50.

You can apply for any particular branch of the service you wish to serve in, and if otherwise suitable will be allotted to that branch. If you wish to serve in the Infantry you will, as far as possible, be given the opportunity of joining the new Regular Battalion of your County Regiment which is being raised for the War.

If you wish to join the Regular Army for longer than the War, there should be no difficulty provided that you are unmarried, your height and chest are as above, and your age is from 18 to 25. Or you might be accepted for the Special Reserve for 6 years if your age is 17 to 30 and height 5 feet 2 inches or over; in the Special Reserve, so long as the War lasts, you would be treated in all respects as a soldier of the Regular Forces, and after the War would only be required to perform a few weeks military training each year so long as your engagement continued.

But the best thing you can do is to enlist *NOW* for the duration of the War, and you can consider the question of transferring for longer service afterwards.

For further information apply to any Military Barrack or Recruiting Office; the addresses of the latter can be obtained from Post Offices or Labour Exchanges.

GOD SAVE THE KING.

Some details of conditions of service offered.

◀ *A recruiting poster. How does the artist appeal to young men to join the army?*

'Join the army.' 'Get your son to join the army.' 'Get your friends to join the army.' These were the answers. But many still did not join.

Andrew Clark was a vicar. He lived in Great Leighs in Essex. He knew everyone in the village. The war office wrote to him. They wanted his help. They wanted to advertise a recruiting march. He wrote back:

> **Source 7.7**
> 'Men will not enlist unless the slackers are made to enlist with them. I am sure the village mind is quite made up.'
>
> Diary entry 13 May 1915.
> From Reverend A. Clark,
> *Echoes of the Great War* (OUP, 1985).

Conscription

In January 1916 a new law was passed. It said that all young men had to fight or do war work.

Some people hated this law. They said it destroyed a man's freedom. Other people said it was fair. Every man should fight for his country.

White feathers

A white feather was a sign of cowardice. Some people handed white feathers to young men who were not in uniform. Do you think this was fair?

About 35 per cent of men were passed as Grade I. When the army was really short of men very few were turned away. Good army food often improved boys of 18. They grew taller and put on weight.

'Great Scott! I must do something. Dashed if I don't get some more flags for the old jigger!' (This cartoon appeared in September 1914.)

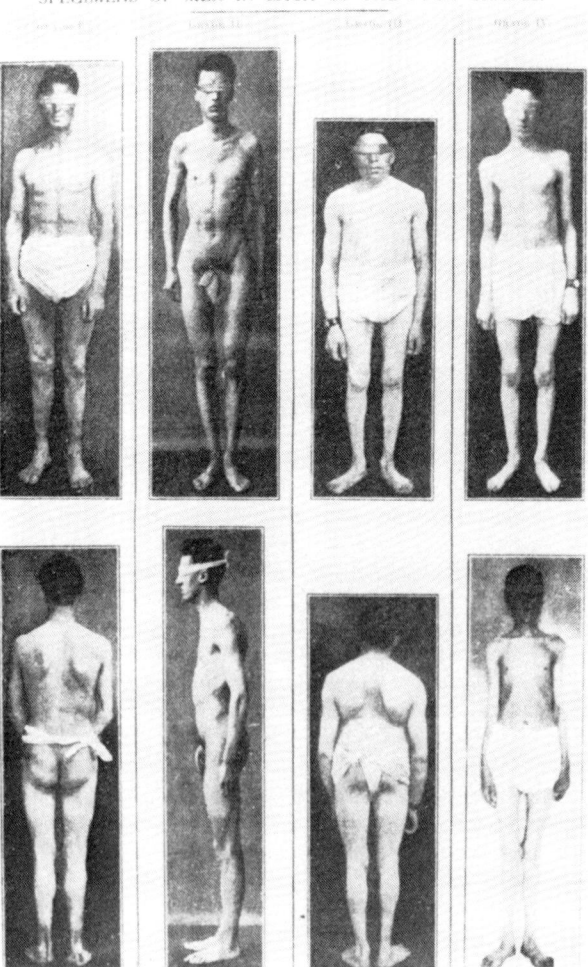

SPECIMENS OF MEN IN EACH OF THE FOUR GRADES.

Things to Do

1. How many men did Lord Kitchener need (lines 1–2)?
2. Read Source 7.4.
   (a) Write out the sentences below. Choose the correct words from the brackets:

   The (colonel/corporal) said that it was (sad/wonderful) to be (80/18). The boys of 18 were (lucky/unlucky). They were England's (rags/riff-raff/rubbish/riches).

   (b) In what way do you think 18-year-old boys were England's riches?
   (c) If a boy was 18 years old in 1914, in what year was he born? How old would he be now?
3. Read Source 7.1. Why did Alfred Blake join the army?
4. Read Source 7.2. Why did Roland Leighton join the army?
5. Read Source 7.6. Who did the writer blame for the war?
6. Do any of the sources in the chapter show that some men were not so keen on the war?
7. Look back over the chapter, at the photographs as well as the writing. Discuss in class or in groups how many different pressures were put on a young man to join the army or navy. If you had been a young man in 1914 what would you have done?

8 Defence of the Realm

DORA

DORA stood for Defence of the Realm Act. This was a law. It was passed by Parliament on 8 August 1914. The law gave the government a great deal of power.

The Houses of Parliament, where the laws of the country are made.

Sea scouts took over many coastguards' jobs. This sea scout is examining a photographer's permit. Why do you think photographers had to have permits?

Source 8.1

'Be it enacted by the King's Most Excellent Majesty by and with the advice and consent of the Lords Spiritual and Temporal, and Commons in this present Parliament assembled and by the authority of the same as follows:

1. His Majesty in Council has power during the continuance of the present war to issue regulations as to the powers and duties of the Admiralty and Army Council and of the members of His Majesty's forces and other persons acting on His behalf, for securing the public safety and the defence of the realm; and may by such regulations authorize the trial by courts martial and punishing of persons contravening any of the provisions of such regulations designed:

   (a) to prevent persons communicating with the enemy or obtaining information for that purpose or any purpose calculated to jeopardize the success of the operations of any of His Majesty's forces or to assist the enemy; or

   (b) to secure the safety of any means of communication, or of railways, docks or harbours

in a like manner as if such persons were subject to military law and had on active service committed an offence under section five of the Army Act....'

This is how a law or Act of Parliament is worded. Do not worry about the difficult words. Look at the section marked 1. This section says that the government has great power to give orders to the navy, the army and anyone else working for the government.

Auckland Rural Food Control Committee. Gravesend in Kent was the first place to try rationing food. Then many other places brought in rationing too. This card is from Bishop Auckland. On the right are the coupons (some have been used). Read the instructions. What is the offence under the Defence of the Realm Acts?

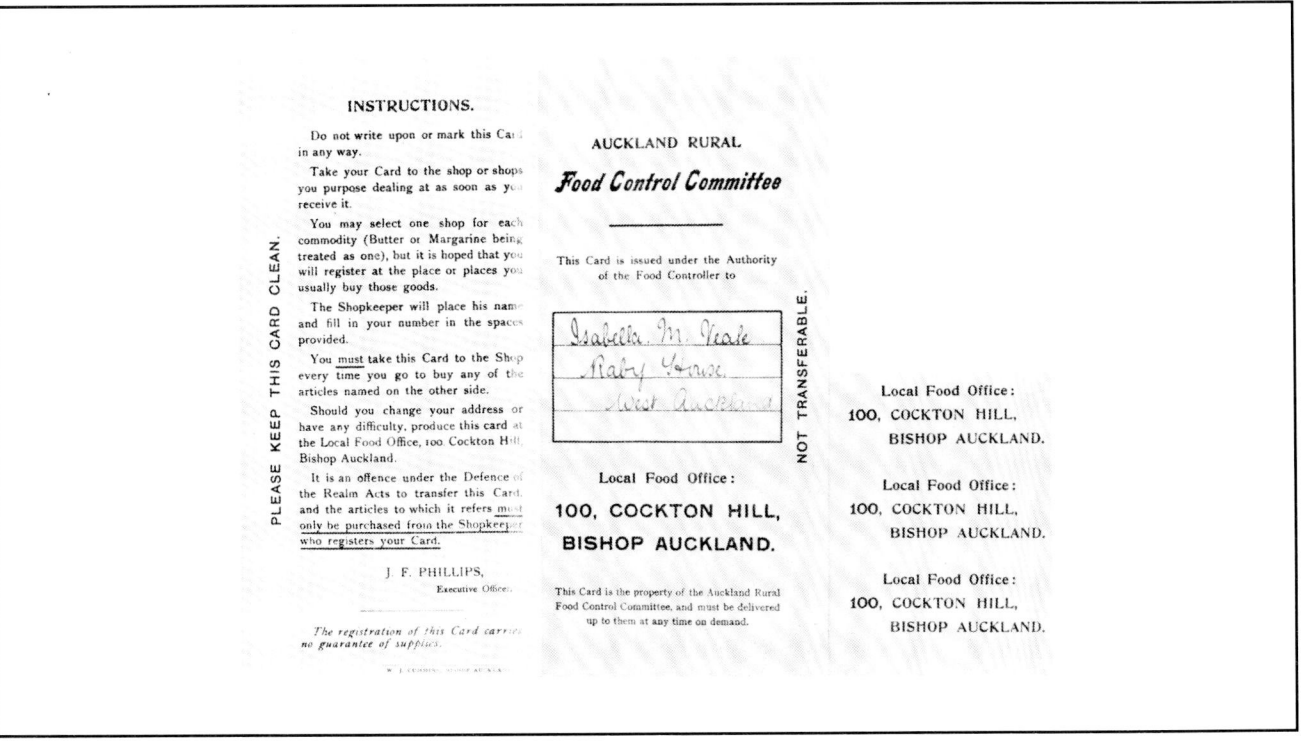

Things to Do

1 Complete this sentence about the power which the Act gave to the government.

The government wanted this power so that it could secure public safety and for the ──────── of the ───── (lines 18–19).

2 What do you think **defence of the realm** means? Choose the meaning that you think is correct from the list below.

building a fence   shooting spies
driving a bus   fighting to save
fighting to get more   your country
   land   defending your own
                 house

3 Look at (a) in Source 8.1. Then choose the sentence that describes what (a) is saying:

- (a) is saying that people working as spies must be stopped.
- (a) is saying that all soldiers must be ready to die for their country.

4 Look at (b) in Source 8.1. Then choose the sentence that describes what (b) is saying:

- (b) is saying that no one is to travel by train.
- (b) is saying that all telephones, radios, roads, railways, docks and harbours must be kept safe.
- (b) is saying that all docks and harbours must be blown up.

5 Discuss in class what sort of trial a soldier *or civilian* faced if he or she broke this law (line 20). How is this different from the trial of a civilian in peace time?

Dorothy Lawrence

Dorothy Lawrence was a young newspaper girl. She made her way to the front line. Disguised as a soldier, she joined some sappers (army engineers). She went mining with them towards the German lines but after ten days was found out. She was sent home. On the boat she met Mrs Pankhurst, the suffragette. Mrs Pankhurst asked Miss Lawrence to talk at a recruiting rally about what she had seen and done.

> **Source 8.2**
>
> 'I found out I couldn't say anything about what I had seen or done at the front. I would be breaking the Defence of the Realm Act.'
>
> From David Mitchell, *Women on the Warpath* (Jonathan Cape, 1965).

THE ENEMY'S ALLY.

'Drink is doing us more damage in the war than all the German submarines put together.' Lloyd George, 28 February 1915.

1. What damage were submarines doing to the British, do you think?
2. Discuss how the artist of the cartoon has made you think drunkenness is evil.
3. Look carefully at the cartoon. What damage do you think Lloyd George is talking about?
4. Why do you think generals and admirals were worried about drunkenness (line 58)?

Drink

Under the Defence of the Realm Act, pubs in ports or near army camps could be made to open for much shorter hours if the generals and admirals wanted the pubs closed.

Shorter hours

These were the opening times for pubs before 1914:

London	5 a.m. to 12.30 p.m.
Country	6 a.m. to 11.00 p.m.
Scotland	10 a.m. to 11.00 p.m.

On Sundays pubs were either closed or open for much shorter times.

Soon all pubs had much shorter opening hours.

Treating

Treating was forbidden.

> *Source 8.3*
>
> ‘"Treating", the custom of buying drinks in rounds, grew into a huge nuisance when many a man saw an easy way of doing his duty by buying drinks for his fellows in uniform.’
>
> From Arthur Marwick, *The Deluge* (Macmillan, 1973).

Weak beer, high prices and profiteering

Beer and spirits were watered down. This was to keep down drunkenness. The watering down meant less grain was needed. This meant ships could bring more important goods to Britain instead.

The price of beer and spirits was put up. This was to control drunkenness. But it also meant that many of the breweries made big profits. The making of big profits was known as profiteering. Many people felt it was bad to make money out of the war. Some people stayed in Britain and got rich, while soldiers were in France dying.

The government did not control prices. The government was a big buyer in the war. For example, the government bought boots for all the soldiers. The big manufacturers who made the boots made huge profits.

Result of control of drink

> *Source 8.4*
> **Weekly convictions for drunkenness in England and Wales**
>
> | | |
> |---|---|
> | 1914 | 3,388 |
> | 1918 | 449 |

> *Source 8.5*
>
> ‘Grocers and other shopkeepers say that they have never done such good business on Saturdays.’
>
> From H. Carter, *The Control of the Drink Trade in Britain* (New York, 1919).

Things to Do

1. What were the pub opening hours in London before 1914 (lines 63–7)?
2. What was 'treating' (lines 73–4)?
3. (a) Look at Source 8.4. Apart from shorter pub hours, what other reasons might there have been for less drunkenness by 1918?
   (b) Read Source 8.5. Why is this source evidence of less drunkenness? Can you think of other reasons for grocers doing better business on Saturdays?
4. Many people were worried that the Defence of the Realm Act gave the government too much power over ordinary people's lives. What do you think people feared? What controls do you think they would have welcomed?
5. Under what section of DORA was Miss Lawrence not allowed to speak?

9 The Women's Peace Conference in the Hague, 1915

It was April 1915. Two thousand women met at the Hague in the Netherlands. The women came from twelve countries. Six of the countries were at war with each other. The women did not discuss how the war started. They did not discuss who was winning. They discussed how to stop the war.

The women's peace conference was held in the Hague in the Netherlands in 1915.

Stop the war

Already over 2 million men had been killed, injured, or taken prisoner. The women sat in the big conference hall. It was filled with flowers and plants. The women could hear the guns booming on the western front. A million men were killing each other.

Austrian, German, British, American women and others talked about the war. They tried to arrange peace talks.

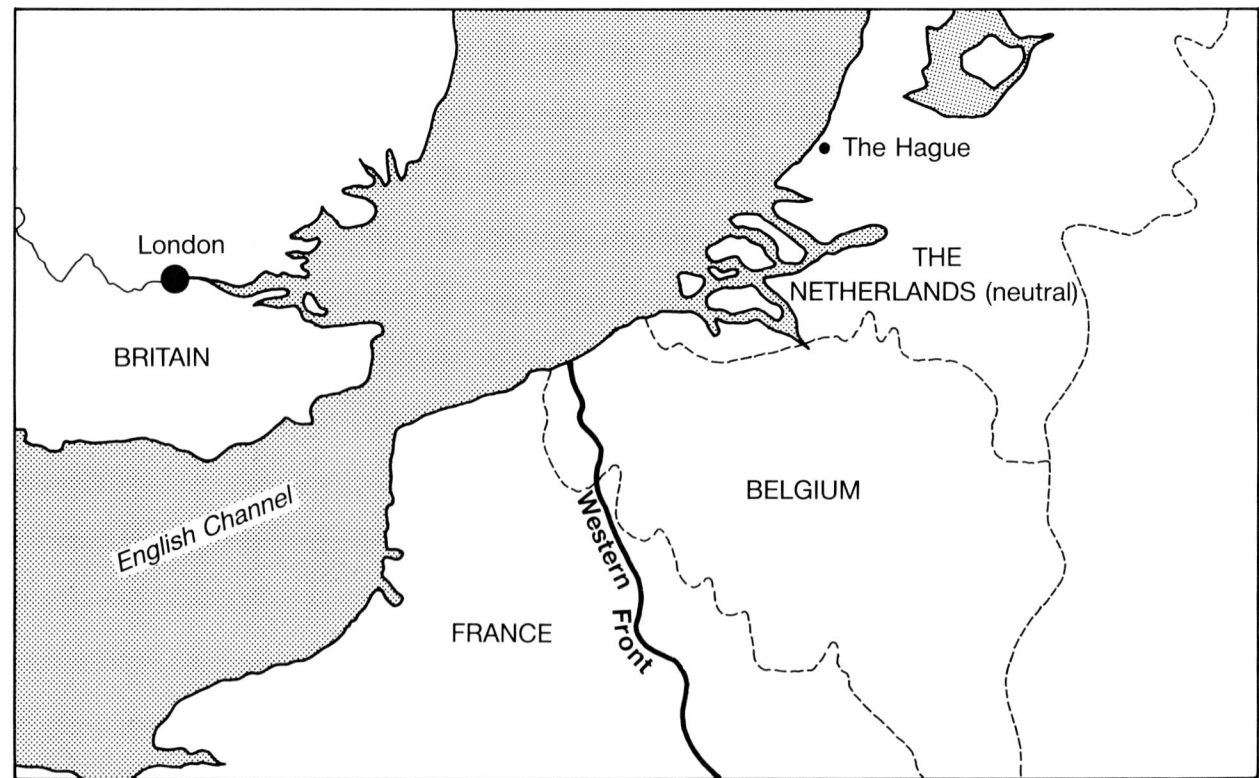

Crystal Macmillan

Crystal Macmillan was a Scottish lawyer. She travelled to Russia and Norway. Other women travelled to Austria and Germany. They spoke to the governments. Everyone agreed to peace talks. They wanted Sweden to start the talks. All the women were excited. They set off for the USA. The USA was powerful. If the American government agreed to help then maybe there would be peace talks.

But the American government did not agree. In July 1915 the Germans sank the *Lusitania*. The *Lusitania* was a big ship. Many Americans were on the ship. So the USA was angry with Germany. It was not interested in helping to arrange peace talks.

No peace

The women's peace movement got nearer to bringing about peace talks than anything else in the First World War. It only just failed. So millions more men died in the war.

Four of the women from the conference went to see the King of Norway to put to him their ideas for peace. Crystal Macmillan is on the left.

34 *The First World War 1914–18*

The Women's Peace Conference, 1915. Many of the women who went belonged to suffrage movements in Europe.

Things to Do

1 From how many countries did the women come (line 3)?
2 What did they discuss (lines 7–8)?
3 Why do you think women, not men, organized the conference?
4 Why was the USA angry with Germany (lines 32–5)?
5 What effect did this anger have on the women's peace movement?
6 Do you think that if women had controlled the governments of the great countries the war would have been stopped?
7 Design a poster for the women's peace conference.

8 Do the crossword. *(Numbers in brackets after some clues refer to text line numbers. You will need to read the whole sentence to find the answer.)*

ACROSS

1 They tried to arrange ------ talks. (18)
3 The women could hear the ---- booming on the western front. (12)
6 They discussed how -- stop the war. (7)
7 Short for Commanding Officer.
8 ---- did not discuss who was winning. (6)
10 --- thousand women met at the Hague in the Netherlands. (1)
12 --- of the countries were at war with each other. (3)
15 So millions more men died in the ---. (41)
16 Two thousand women met -- the Hague in the Netherlands. (1)
18 But the American government did --- agree. (31)
20 The women sat -- the big conference hall. (10)
21 Already over 2 million men had been ------, injured or taken prisoner. (9)
22 Six of the countries were at war with ---- other. (3)

DOWN

2 ------- Macmillan was a Scottish lawyer. (20)
3 The women's peace movement --- nearer to bringing about peace talks than anything else in the First World War. (38)
4 Short for Non Commissioned Officer.
5 -- millions more men died in the war. (41)
9 Already over 2 million men --- been killed, injured or taken prisoner. (9)
11 The ----- did not discuss how the war started. (5)
13 Austrian, German, ------- and American women and others talked about the war. (16)
14 Everyone agreed to peace ------. (24)
17 They --- not discuss who was winning. (6)
19 --- the women were excited. (26)

10 Rumours

For many years before 1914 Britain was afraid of Germany. Germany grew richer. It built more ships. It wanted more land. It wanted an empire. Britain had an empire. Did Germany want to take some of Britain's empire? Britain was worried. People wrote adventure stories. They wrote spy stories. The enemy was always Germany.

War

By 1914 British people were used to the idea of a war with Germany. This was dangerous. The Archduke Franz Ferdinand was shot on 28 June. His death started a row among the great countries of Europe. Britain did not feel involved. It was not thinking about war. But suddenly Germany attacked Belgium. Britain felt it must help Belgium. British people felt the Germans had gone too far. They were wicked to attack Belgium. So British people were keen to fight the Germans.

Atrocity stories

The British decided the Germans were evil. The Germans did dreadful things, they said. You could read about the dreadful things they did in the newspapers. These were rumours.

Rumours

Everyone was afraid of spies. The government was afraid of spies. The government decided to tell the newspapers nothing about the war. But people wanted to know. They read news pinned up in post office windows.

A cartoonist's view of the spy scare in 1914. 'Nurse: "Goodness me! What 'ave you been doing to your dolls?" Joan: "Charlie's killed them! He said they were made in Germany, and how were we to know they weren't spies?"'

How rumours start. 'Nurse: "I wonder if that man's a German spy."' (This cartoon appeared in November 1914.)

Source 10.1

'OFFICIAL WAR NEWS – Sunday 16 August 1914. German plan of invading France seriously delayed by resistance at Liège and fighting with French cavalry. So French have carried out mobilization and concentration. Some Belgian and French successes reported.
NO BRITISH CASUALTIES.'

So who was winning? Who was losing? People wanted to know more. They talked to each other about the war. This led to rumours.

The Russian soldiers

One rumour was about Russian soldiers. Russia was Britain's ally. It was sending soldiers to help. People said that thousands of Russian soldiers had landed in Scotland. Some were marching down through Britain. Some were travelling in trains. Everyone knew they were Russians. They still had snow on their boots! Many people knew someone who had seen them.

Other rumours

There were thousands of other rumours. People were scared of invasion by the Germans, scared of zeppelins, scared of spies.

Source 10.2

'Here is a German spy story told to me today. In Braintree there was a cook, but she went out to dinner at the White Hart Hotel. She was dressed as a woman but had very large feet, so was probably a man. She said that zeppelins would come to Braintree and to Scotland. It has all turned out as she said. She was certainly a spy.'

From Reverend A. Clark, *Echoes of the Great War* (OUP, 1985).

Sometimes people made a joke of what they weren't told. (This cartoon appeared in November 1914.)

Censorship

The government kept quiet about the fighting. They also kept journalists away from the front line. Letters from soldiers were censored. Here is a letter that a soldier might have written from the western front:

Dear Mum and Dad,
The weather is very cold but with any luck we will not be in these trenches much longer. We are due to move back into rest on the 17th. We're going to be replaced by a Scottish regiment and they are pretty fierce so the Germans had better watch out!

Our trenches here are about six feet deep and well fortified but we have trouble with earth slipping in wet weather. Nobody has cured this yet and we are short of sandbags.

I hope you are keeping well.

Love from
Bob

This letter might fall into German hands before it could be sent back to Britain. The Germans would learn a lot from a letter like this. So an officer censored it. That is, he crossed out everything that might help the Germans.

The problem

The government could tell people everything. Then German spies would know too. (Secondly, everyone would know about the government's mistakes in the war!) Thirdly, the British might panic. For example, German submarines sank many British ships. In April 1917 there was only six weeks' food left in Britain. If the government told you this through the newspapers what would you do? What would everyone else do? What might happen?

But rumours were as bad so the government had to give some information.

Photographs like this were either not allowed to be printed so that the British did not know that the Germans had had a successful raid, or they were used as propaganda. How would you use this photograph for propaganda? Suppression of information led to more rumours.

40 *The First World War 1914–18*

Things to Do

1 Fill in the gaps. *(Numbers in brackets refer to text line numbers.)*

Everyone was afraid of ----- (28). The government was ------ (29) of spies. The government decided to tell the ---------- (31) nothing about the --- (31). But ------ (32) wanted to know. They talked to each other about the war. This led to rumours.

2 Sources 10.3–10.6 are four newspaper accounts of what happened when the Germans captured Antwerp. Read them carefully.

Source 10.3

'When the fall of Antwerp became known the church bells were rung in Germany.'

From the German newspaper *Kölnische Zeitung*.

Source 10.4

'According to the *Kölnische Zeitung*, the priests of Antwerp were forced to ring the church bells when the fortress of Antwerp fell.'

From the French newspaper *Le Matin*.

Source 10.5

'According to what *The Times* has heard from Cologne via Paris, the poor Belgian priests who refused to ring the church bells when Antwerp was taken, have been sentenced to hard labour.'

From the Italian newspaper *Corriere della Sera*.

Source 10.6

'According to the *Corriere della Sera*, from Cologne via London, it is confirmed that the barbaric Germans punished the Belgian priests who refused to ring the church bells by hanging them, as living clappers to the bells, with their heads down.'

From *Le Matin*.

(a) Look at Source 10.3. Where were the church bells rung?
(b) Look at Source 10.4. Where were the church bells rung? What else has been changed or added?
(c) Look at Source 10.5. What has been changed or added?
(d) Look at Source 10.6. What has been changed or added? Now look back at Source 10.3. Do you see how much has changed?
(e) Why do you think the story changed?

3 Make a rumour. One person (A) thinks of an incident she or he has seen – on television, in a local shop, in the street. The person A goes outside the classroom and tells one other member (B) of the class. Then A goes back into the class. B then tells C. C tells D and so on. Ask the last person to say what happened. Compare it to what A said happened.

4 Write briefly *your* opinion of any or all of the following:

the USA
a rival school
Germany
Britain
your local village
London
MI5
a soap opera
you don't watch
the prime minister
the police

Ask yourself how you found out about the topic you have chosen (someone told you, from the television, newspapers, from your parents, etc.). How reliable is the evidence that your opinion is based on?

5 Look again at Bob's letter to his parents (lines 74–87). Imagine that you are working as a British censor in France.

Then discuss the following questions in class:

(a) What would you cross out in the letter?
(b) How much would be left?
(c) How much would Bob's parents know about what was happening when they finally got the letter?

11 Women in Uniform and Outside the Home

Source 11.1

'The great searchlight of war showed things in their true light. They gave us enfranchisement with open hands.'

M. Garrett Fawcett, January 1918.

Is the writer a man or a woman? What is enfranchisement? Who was given enfranchisement in 1918? Talk about this in class.

Women's war work

The Great War started in 1914. Thousands of young men went to fight. Many were wounded. The wounded men needed nursing.

Voluntary Aid Detachments

The Voluntary Aid Detachments were run partly by the Red Cross. Many girls joined. They were called VADs. Many VADs nursed soldiers. They worked with fully trained nurses.

Source 11.2

'We went on duty at 7.30 a.m. and came off at 8 p.m., including three hours off time and a weekly half day.'

From Vera Brittain, *Testament of Youth* (Victor Gollancz, 1933).

This was a terrific shock to girls from comfortable homes. The long hours and the dreadful wounds were hard to bear. But the good thing was the freedom. The young nurses and other war workers could go out alone with a young man. They did not have to have a chaperone or an older woman with them all the time.

◀ A Woman's Weekly *magazine cover. How does this picture compare with descriptions of real-life nursing (lines 17–35)?*

Nursing

> **Source 11.3**
>
> ‘The first dressing at which I assisted – a gangrenous leg wound, slimy and green and scarlet, with the bone laid bare – turned me sick and faint for a moment.’
>
> From Vera Brittain, *Testament of Youth* (Victor Gollancz, 1933).

Vera Brittain soon got used to the long hours. She got used to her cold lodgings. She got used to the long, early morning walk to the hospital. But she was horrified when the battle of the Somme started. The nurses knew a big battle was coming. They were told to get the beds ready. There were rows and rows of empty beds. They were waiting for the hospital ships to bring the wounded men back to Britain.

Other women in uniform

Apart from nurses, school girls and domestic servants, women did not wear uniforms before the First World War. But now thousands of women put on uniforms. Women police patrols started. Women firefighters worked beside men. By 1917 the army and the navy accepted women.

Women's Army Auxiliary Corps

The Women's Army Auxiliary Corps (WAAC) helped to run the army. The WAACs took over men's jobs in army offices. Then the men could go and fight. By November 1918 there were over 8,000 WAACs with the army abroad. There were over 31,000 WAACs with the army in Britain. Two years after the war ended the WAACs were disbanded.

An instructor of the WRNS demonstrating how to use gas respirators.

The women's police force was started.

Women horse trainers in the army. This mule is being taught to 'foot up'. This stopped it from kicking when being harnessed.

Source 11.4
Some of the main jobs of women working outside the home

	1914	1918
Munitions	212,000	947,000
Transport	18,200	117,200
Commerce	505,200	934,500
Agriculture	190,000	228,000
Government and teaching	262,200	460,200
Hotels, etc.	181,000	220,000
Industry	2,178,600	2,970,600
Domestic service	1,658,000	1,250,000
Self-employed	430,000	470,000
Nursing, secretarial (does not include VADs)	542,000	652,500

A tramway conductress. Glasgow Corporation started employing women as conductors and in the workshops in 1915. It employed 1,633 conductresses. The women earned 45s 8d (£2.28) a week and worked 51 hours a week.

Things to Do

1. Look at Source 11.4. Which job lost women workers between 1914 and 1918? Give reasons for your answer.
2. Which job gained most women workers? Give reasons for your answer.
3. Choose five sets of figures from the table in Source 11.4. Use a scale of
   👤 = 100,000 women
   Show the sets of figures you have chosen as drawings of women. For example:
   Self-employed
   1914 👤👤👤👤👤   1918 👤👤👤👤👤
4. How many types of job are mentioned in Chapter 11?
5. Many women had not worked outside the home before the war. What new skills did women learn? Use the text in the chapter and Source 11.4.
6. Why was it difficult for anyone to say that women could not have the vote (be enfranchised) after the war?
7. Look at Sources 11.2 and 11.3.
   Like many young women in the armed services or working as VADs, Vera Brittain went home to her parents when the war ended. Make up a conversation between an ex-VAD and her parents discussing what she is going to do next. The following ideas may help:

   - staying at home with her parents
   - enfranchisement for women
   - her brother and many of his friends are dead
   - settling down
   - fewer jobs available after the war
   - getting married
   - working as a housemaid in a big house

12 To Fight or Not to Fight

In 1916 Parliament passed the Military Service Act. Single men aged between 18 and 40 had to join the army, the navy, or the air force.

At first married men did not have to join up. Many people thought that was unfair. Soon married men had to join up too.

Tribunals

Some men did important jobs. For instance, an engine driver drove steam trains. Britain still needed trains. So engine drivers did not have to join up.

Britain needed coal. So coal miners did not have to join up.

The government set up tribunals. There were thousands of tribunals in Britain. Men could appeal to the tribunals. They could say why they could not go to fight. Sources 12.1–12.6 list some of the reasons men gave to tribunals:

> *Source 12.1*
>
> 'I am a tripe dresser. I cut the lining from cows' stomachs, therefore I produce essential food. *My* job is too revolting for a woman to do.'
>
> Report by Harold Cartmell, Preston. From E. S. Turner, *Dear Old Blighty* (Michael Joseph, 1980).

> *Source 12.2*
>
> 'My son is my eleventh son. The other ten are serving in France. Five have been wounded and two are prisoners. I do not want my eleventh son to leave me too.'
>
> From E. S. Turner, *Dear Old Blighty* (Michael Joseph, 1980).

> *Source 12.3*
>
> 'Richard Arnold asked to keep his farm man called Wells because:
> "(a) Wells is the man who looks after my sheep. If he were taken away I must sell my sheep and then there would be only one flock in the parish.
> (b) Wells has four young children and if he were killed the country would have a long time to keep them."'
>
> Diary entry for Tuesday 11 July 1916.
> From Reverend A. Clark, *Echoes of the Great War* (OUP, 1985).

> *Source 12.4*
>
> 'Alix Alefounder had asthma and bronchitis. The villagers say he could not walk up a hill fast to save his life.'
>
> Diary entry for Friday 9 June 1916.
> From Reverend A. Clark, *Echoes of the Great War* (OUP, 1985).

> *Source 12.5*
>
> 'Albert Wright is the only man on the farm who can drive the new motor plough.'
>
> From Reverend A. Clark, *Echoes of the Great War* (OUP, 1985).

> *Source 12.6*
>
> 'John had a conscientious objection to taking human life and would not do anything to help in the war.'
>
> From J. Bell, *We Did Not Fight* (1933).

Imagine you were on the local tribunal. Which men would you allow to stay at home and not join the army, the navy or the air force? (The tribunals who listened to the different stories allowed the men in Sources 12.2–12.5 to stay at home. Why do you think the men in Sources 12.1 and 12.6 were told they had to join the army?)

Conscientious objectors

Some people believed that war was wrong. They believed this very strongly. They would not fight.

The men and women on the tribunals listened carefully. They had to decide. Was the man just trying to get out of fighting? Or was he really against war?

Some conscientious objectors went to work on farms and in forests. Some men became ambulance workers but some men refused to do anything to help the war. Many of them went to prison. People jeered at them. Some conscientious objectors were badly treated.

Peace

Conscientious objectors believed that people should not kill each other. They did not believe in war.

'*April 1917. Working for the camera. The Dartmoor conscientious objectors are here seen supposedly tilling the soil, but they spend much of their time "on leave" or "in strolling on the moors, smoking, reading, and talking".*'
This caption appeared on the back of this photograph from a photo library.

1 Is the writer sympathetic to conscientious objectors?
2 How would you feel if you read this caption in a newspaper and your son was a soldier on the Western Front?
3 Now imagine your son was a conscientious objector and write your own caption for the photograph.

Things to Do

1 Fill in the gaps. (*Numbers in brackets refer to text line numbers.*)

In ———— (1) Parliament passed the Military ——————— (2) Act. Single ——— (2) between 18 and —— (3) had to join the army, the ———— (3) or the ——— force (4).

2 Set up your own tribunal in class. Between five and twenty-five men and women sat on a tribunal. They would be important local people – doctors, well-to-do farmers, magistrates, and so on. They were not supposed to know about the law in detail. They had to use their common sense. A military adviser (usually a retired officer) sat with them. He was not to make decisions. His job was to advise the tribunal on the new Military Service Act and on military matters. For example, he would give advice on whether a man with an injured left hand and mild asthma was going to be useful in the army, or would spend more time in hospital than fighting. Below are some cases for you to decide on. All these men had asked to be excused from joining the army for the following reasons:

(a) 'I make clogs. Mill workers must have clogs.'
(b) 'I can skin 1,200 rabbits overnight and kill, pluck and prepare a chicken for market in two minutes.'
(c) 'I am a cowman. I am more use milking cows than I would be in the army.'
(d) 'I will not take life. I am a vegetarian and a pacifist.'
(e) 'I am a coal miner. I work at the coal face.'

13 Propaganda

Every piece of news about the war was censored. So British people believed in rumours. Sometimes they panicked. But more and more they demanded to know what was going on. At the battle of the Somme the newspapers had headlines about great British victories. Yet within a few days the casualty lists were huge. What was really going on?

The government

The government realized that it must give some information. So it worked hard to give the information that it wanted the British people to have. The government still kept newspaper reporters away from the front line fighting as much as possible. But it gave more official news.

Keeping the fighting going

The war dragged on. Neither side would give in. Each side thought that it might win.

The governments had to keep their people keen on the war. So they had to keep them hating the enemy. They had to keep them loving their own soldiers. Most British people were happy to keep supporting the war. Everything they read or were told kept them that way.

Lord Northcliffe owned newspapers. He whipped up hatred for Germany. Other newspapers carried cartoons of dreadful Germans. There were posters too.

Things to Do

1 Look carefully at the illustrations in this chapter. Look through the book and decide which pictures in other chapters might also be propaganda pictures.
2 There are few photographs of conscientious objectors. The Imperial War Museum, which holds the official war photographs, has none of conscientious objectors or of food queues. Why do you think this is?

(Top left) A poster issued by the Essex County Recruiting Committee. Edith Cavell was a nurse in Belgium during the war. She was executed by the Germans for helping their enemies, the British. In what ways has the Essex County Recruiting Committee used the story of Edith Cavell?

(Lower left) An Australian recruiting poster using the same means as the British to keep alive hatred of Germany.

(Top right) Many photographs were taken of children injured in air raids in Britain. Why do you think this was?

(Lower right) A Punch *cartoon of a U-boat captain. How does this cartoon work to whip up British hatred for Germans?*

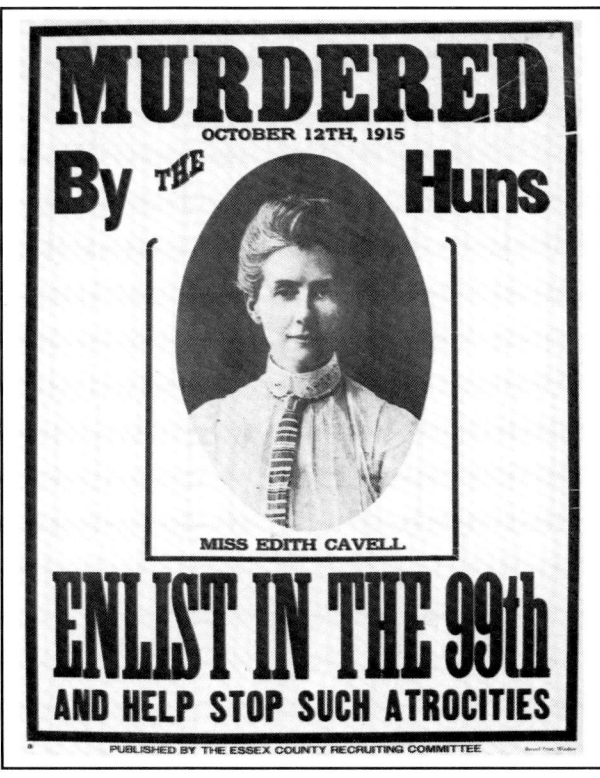

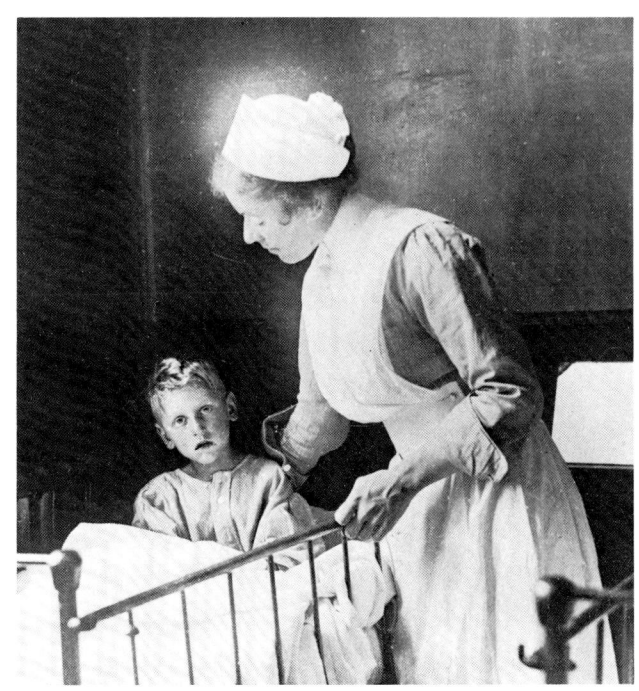

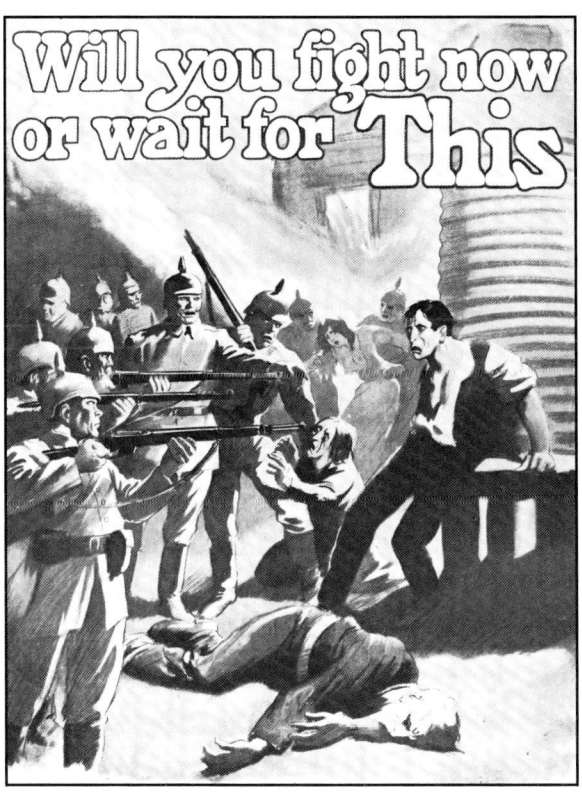

A GREAT NAVAL TRIUMPH.

50 The First World War 1914–18

This cartoon appeared in 1915. Prussia was part of Germany.

STUDY OF A PRUSSIAN HOUSEHOLD HAVING ITS MORNING HATE.

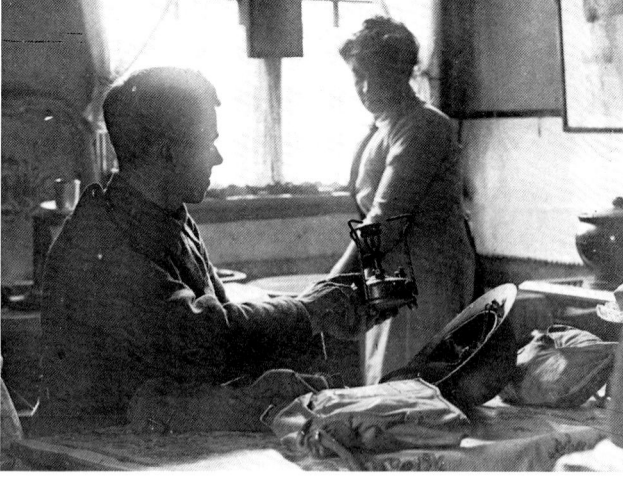

A soldier and his mother. These two pictures are part of a set of official photographs called 'telling the story', which shows a soldier home on leave. The photos show how proud the soldier was of his uniform, of telling about the fighting and the glory. They are all posed, and were laughed at by many soldiers. Why did the government have these photographs taken?

14 Wounded Soldiers

Walking wounded

Source 14.1

'I remember thinking how untidy the battlefield was. There were hundreds of bodies. There were torn and bloody bandages, burst haversacks, rifles driven muzzle first into the mud to mark a body. And paper – torn paper, letters, postcards, wrappings from parcels. I still felt no pain but I was so tired.'

S. Cloete. From Denis Winter, *Death's Men: Soldiers of the Great War* (Allen Lane, 1978).

Cloete walked slowly back to the regimental first aid post. He was wounded. He was out of it. He was no longer part of the battle around him.

An advanced dressing station, September 1916.
1. How is it protected?
2. What are piled up in the centre foreground?
3. Find the rifle with the bayonet still fixed.
4. What other items can you see in the photograph?

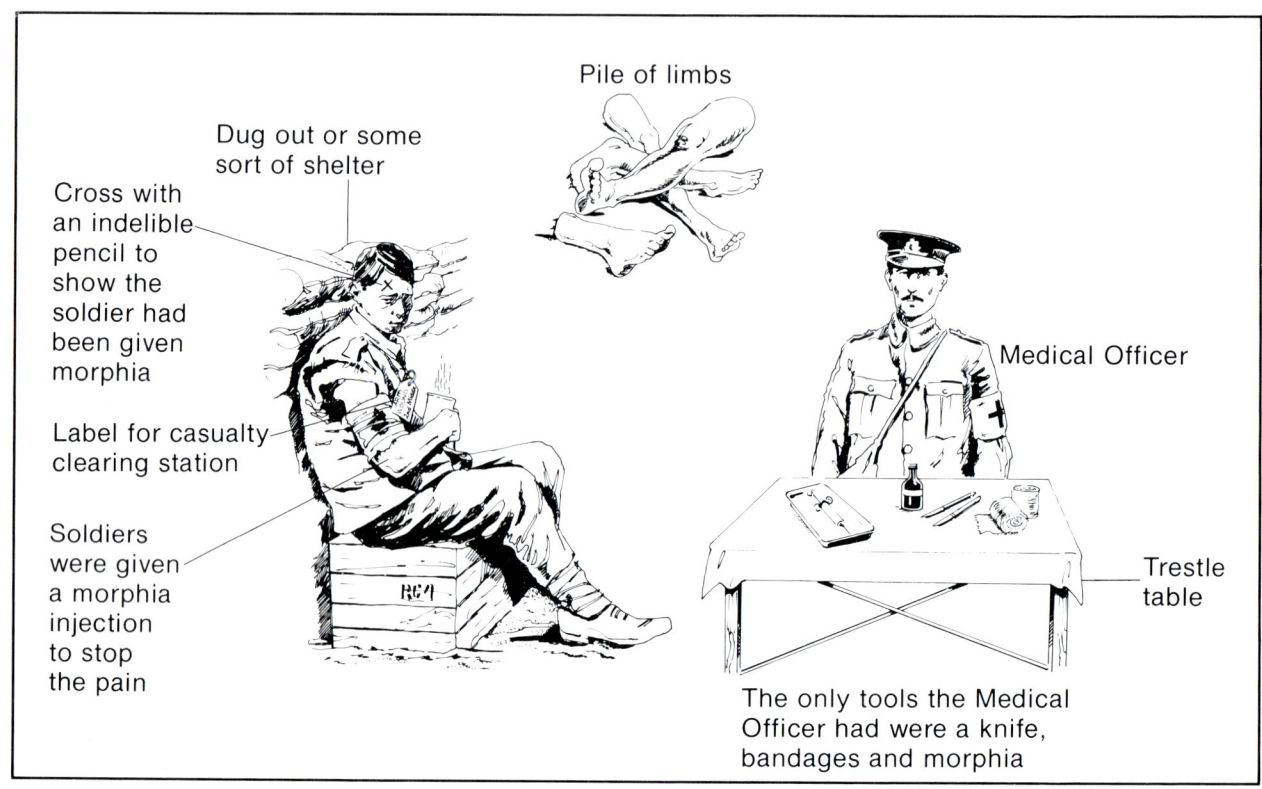

A regimental first aid post.

Regimental first aid post

The regimental first aid post was in a reserve trench, a dugout or a shellhole. It was as near the fighting as possible. Some wounds were not serious. The men were bandaged. They went back to the front line. To get a wound stripe (a gold stripe to sew on your tunic) you had to be wounded badly enough to be out of the fighting line for fourteen days.

A wounded soldier had no kit. He was allowed to dump his kit as soon as he was wounded.

Casualty clearing station

Wounded soldiers went from the regimental first aid post to the casualty clearing station. This was run by the Royal Army Medical Corps (RAMC). Source 14.2 will give you an idea of the thousands of men injured between 1914 and 1918.

Source 14.2

	Wounded	Killed
Expected casualties in a battle	60%	12%
Number of men and women working for the Royal Army Medical Corps by 1918	150,000	
Number of beds in RAMC hospitals	500,000	
Number of wounded and ill men cared for 1914–18	9,000,000	
Doses of drugs given 1914–18	1,088,000,000	
Splints 1914–18	1,500,000	
Number of bandages (each bandage was 2 metres long)	108,000,000	
Cotton wool in tonnes	7,250	
Artificial eyes	22,386	

Nine million men were operated on or patched up in casualty clearing stations. There were many casualty clearing stations. A badly wounded soldier had injured or dead flesh around his wound. It could go bad. He then got gangrene or sepsis and rotted to death. There were no drugs like antibiotics to help him. All the injured and dead flesh had to be cut away. The surgeons at the casualty clearing stations worked desperately. They operated in tents lit by acetylene flares. They were helped by nurses and anaesthetists. They operated on twenty men at a time. The men were caked with mud, blood and sweat from the battlefield. If a surgeon could cut away all dead and injured flesh within 30 hours of the soldier being wounded, he stood a much better chance of living.

The seriously wounded

Seriously wounded men were sent back to base hospital or to Britain. Most travelled by train, in bunks along the sides of the train.

Of the 9 million wounded men, $2\frac{1}{4}$ million were sent back to Britain.

The battle of the Somme, 1 July 1916

Back in Britain people waited. Nurses and doctors waited.

Vera Brittain was a VAD nurse at hospital in Camberwell.

> *Source 14.3*
>
> ‘ At the end of June the hospital had orders to clear out all convalescents, and prepare for the rush of wounded. ’
>
> From Vera Brittain, *Testament of Youth* (Victor Gollancz, 1933).

She wondered desperately about her brother Edward. On 1 July all the beds were ready. Vera and a friend were given

Nurses auctioning a German helmet on board a hospital barge. Most wounded men travelled by train to the ships that were to take them to Britain. Those who travelled by barge found it very restful. These soldiers do not seem to be badly wounded.

the afternoon off, the last for a long time. They went to the cathedral.

> *Source 14.4*
>
> ‘ We came out from the dim peace to the shouting and saw newspaper boys with huge posters running up and down. I clutched Betty's arm.
>
> "GREAT BRITISH OFFENSIVE BEGINS." ’
>
> From Vera Brittain, *Testament of Youth* (Victor Gollancz, 1933).

The days passed. No word from Edward. Vera lived in dread of a telegram to say he was dead. Then the convoys of ambulances began to arrive. That very morning Vera went to the letter rack in the hospital.

Source 14.5

> I saw a crushed, pencil scrawled envelope in Edward's handwriting – at least he couldn't be dead! I pulled it down but even then I could hardly open it, for the paper was so thin and my fingers shook so. The words were faint and uneven.
>   "Dear Vera, I was wounded in the action this morning in left arm and right thigh not seriously. Hope to come to England. Don't worry, Edward."
>   For a moment the room spun.

From Vera Brittain, *Testament of Youth* (Victor Gollancz, 1933).

Then it was back to work, and the ambulances rolled up to the hospital day after day. Vera never got used to seeing the covered stretchers carried into the ward. Was it death, or agony or terrible wounds under that brown blanket? But Edward was safe and by a chance in hundreds he turned up at her hospital in J Ward. She was allowed to rush over and visit him as soon as he arrived. He was sitting up in bed looking cheerful and trying to eat a poached egg with one hand.

Wounded soldiers arriving at Charing Cross Hospital (from Charing Cross Station), September 1914. Later in the war these journeys only took place at night so as to hide the huge number of wounded soldiers from the public.

Things to Do

1. Read Source 14.1. What did a battlefield look like? Write two sentences.
2. Look at Source 14.2.
   (a) Out of every 100 soldiers how many would probably be casualties in a battle?
   (b) How many bandages were used?
   (c) How much cotton wool was used?
3. If the First World War was fought now how different would the medical care be? Write a paragraph.
4. How do you think Vera Brittain felt when she heard from her brother? Write a short note from Vera to her brother replying to his note.

15 Munitions and Women

It was 1915. The government was worried. The war was going to go on and on. It was not going to be over quickly. More and more guns and more and more shells were needed.

David Lloyd George was the first minister of munitions. His job was to make sure that the soldiers had plenty of shells for their guns.

It was the first day of the battle of the Somme. The British guns stood wheel to wheel. The guns stretched for 18 miles. These guns fired thousands and thousands of shells.

People made these shells. They worked in munitions factories in Britain.

Woolwich Arsenal

Woolwich Arsenal was enormous. In 1914, 14,000 men worked there. In 1916, 100,000 people worked there. Half of them were women. They made shells for the guns.

Munition workers from the tailors' shop leaving Woolwich Arsenal by the 4th Gate.

Gunners in Mametz Valley during the battle of the Somme, 1916.

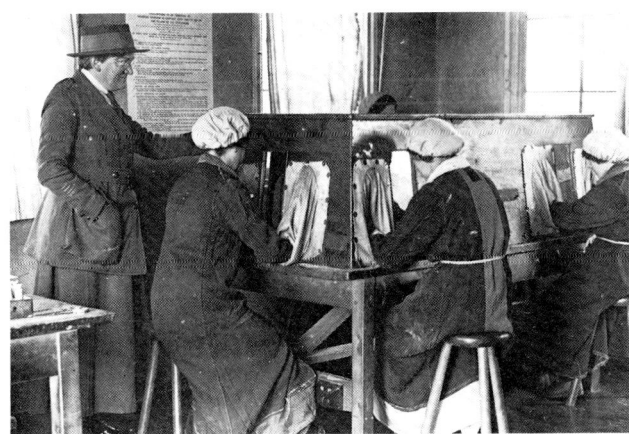

TNT shop at Woolwich Arsenal showing workers with welfare officer Lilian Barker. Women inspectors were appointed to look after women in the factories.

56 *The First World War 1914–18*

Women in the factories

Most women had always worked. They had worked as domestic servants or in their own homes. Housework was very heavy work in those days. Often poor women did extra work outside the home. Women were usually very badly paid. The First World War gave them a new chance for better paid work. But it was not easy.

Attitudes to women were very fixed. Most men thought that women were weak. They thought women did not understand machines and that women were less intelligent. Women went to work in factories. They met all these attitudes and were always paid less than men for the same job. But working class women and girls welcomed work in such places as the munitions factories. It gave them a wage. It meant independence. It was much better than working as living-in housemaid, for example.

But skilled workmen were afraid.

> **Source 15.1**
>
> ' I could quite see it was hard on the men to have women coming into all their pet jobs and in some cases doing them better and I sympathized with the way they were torn between not wanting women to undercut them, and yet hating women to earn as much as them. '
>
> From the *Leeds Mercury*, 23 April 1919.

There were all sorts of ways of paying women lower wages.

> **Source 15.2**
>
> ' I was first put on to a facing machine, turning and facing a part of the fuse cap for one of the big shells. Then I was put on a capstan lathe and performed six operations in all, but it was still unskilled work. '
>
> From Peggy Hamilton, *Three Years or the Duration* (Peter Owen, 1978).

The inside of a howitzer workshop.

Munitions and Women 57

Employers too did not want to pay women much money.

Source 15.3

'With one firm the men are paid full time during a zeppelin raid while the women are not. At another firm the women were employed part on shell and part on fuse making. They were paid as fuse makers only. This was women's work so they were paid lower wages.'

Barbara Drake, *Southampton Times*, 20 March 1919.

◀ Women operating cranes in a shell filling factory at Chilwell, Nottingham. The women climbed a rope to get into the cabs. Then they pulled up the rope. The chains had short jibs with chains and hooks hanging from them. The hooks were fitted into the rings on the noses of the shells by floor workers. Each crane lifted about twelve shells and moved them across the huge building for packing in crates.

Sometimes there was bad feeling. Peggy Hamilton became a skilled munitions worker. She worked the night shift at the London and Scottish Engineering Company. If she did not take home the light bulb she used and the tools at the end of her shift they were missing in the morning.

But there were funny times too.

Source 15.4

'My fitter Bert looked after a number of machines. When all was working well he had nothing to do. He would amuse us and himself. Bert would sit on an upturned box in front of a row of drills and pretend to be playing the organ. He would work into a frenzy of playing. Then the next minute he would be a glamorous lady at her dressing table. He used to make us laugh so much.'

From Peggy Hamilton, *Three Years or the Duration* (Peter Owen, 1978).

Conscription or exemption

From 1916 all fit men could be called up to join the army or the navy. But workers were still needed in the coal mines, on the railways and in the munition factories. Some of the jobs were taken over by women. Some were taken over by men who were not fit enough for the army. Some skilled men were not allowed to join the army. They were too useful in their jobs in Britain.

Source 15.5

'There is great pressure put on men in this district to go munition-working. George Stokes, blacksmith, has to go this week. H.W. Thorogood, landlord of the 'Dog and Partidge', has also had to go. James Humphreys has obtained exemption from military service on condition of munition working.'

Diary entry for 25 April 1917. From Reverend A. Clark, *Echoes of the Great War* (OUP, 1985).

Dangerous work

> **Source 15.6.**
> 'Mabel Lethbridge volunteered for service in the danger zone where high explosives were poured and packed into shells. She worked a machine that forced amatol and TNT down into the eighteen pounder shell cases. Four girls hauled on a rope to raise a massive weight then at a signal let it drop on the mixture until it was packed tight.'
>
> From D. Mitchell, *Women on the Warpath* (Jonathan Cape, no date).

105

Things to Do

1 Read Source 15.1.
   (a) What does undercut mean?
   (b) In what ways were the men torn about women working with them?

2 Read Source 15.3
   (a) How did employers avoid paying women as much as men? Find two ways.
   (b) Why do you think employers tried to pay women less money? (Think carefully. There could be more than one reason.)
   (c) Does this sort of discrimination happen nowadays? Give reasons for your answer.

3 Many of the workmen in the factories had gone to work when they were 12 or 13 years old. It had taken years before they got better jobs as skilled machine workers or foremen. This was because there were so many workers. Then war came. Women came into the factories. They learnt quickly. Many men were fed up that girls could be given jobs it had taken men years to get.

Make up a conversation between a man and a woman in a munitions factory. The man is arguing for lower pay for women. The woman is arguing for equal pay. Try doing this work in a group. Get as many arguments as possible for each side. Try to remember other things you have read in this book and elsewhere about women and their position in society then.

16 Prisoners of War

Each side took prisoners of war. They kept the prisoners in camps. The prisoners often worked. Many soldiers were prisoners for years.

Source 16.1

❛The German prisoners are hard at work on the aerodrome at Chelmsford. They have quarters in the union workhouse and are marched back there from their work about 4.30 p.m. each day. They are said to be very happy, laughing and joking with each other as they pass along the streets. Several Chelmsford girls have been taken before the magistrates for giving them stamps and chocolate.❜

Diary entry for 4 March 1918.
From Reverend A. Clark,
Echoes of the Great War (OUP, 1985).

Leonard Thompson

Leonard was taken prisoner at the battle of Arras in 1917.

Source 16.2

❛After the parade about 300 of us were packed into a half-built mansion and there we lived on pearl barley boiled in coppers and bread or cake made of weed-seed. Then we were put into a forest to make charcoal and sometimes the Germans shot into our legs as we marched.❜

From Ronald Blythe, *Akenfield*
(Allen Lane, 1969).

German prison camp orchestra. PoWs wore uniform at all times. There were other camps for German internees, such as Alexandra Palace.

German PoWs with women who worked at the tailoring factory in London which made German uniforms for German PoWs and British uniforms to send to Germany for British PoWs.

German civilians in Britain

Before the war many German people lived and worked in Britain. Germans worked as waiters. Some Germans ran shops. Some Germans were students. Some were businessmen. Then the war came. The British hated Germany. There were letters in the newspapers about German spies. Some people threw stones at dachschund dogs. German people in Britain left or were interned (kept) in camps for the rest of the war.

Some British people had come from Germany a long time ago. They still had German names although they were British. Many of them changed their names. If they did not they might be attacked or shouted at.

The royal family changed its name from Saxe Coburg to Windsor. Street names that sounded German were changed.

British civilians in Germany

Many British people lived and worked in Germany. The Germans arrested all 4,500 of them in November 1914. They were interned in a camp called Ruhleben for the rest of war.

The British were allowed to organize themselves. They ran their own postal service in the camp. They ran sports events, concerts and plays. They had lectures and classes, a gardening club and a market.

They wrote home to their families in Britain. Their families wrote back and sent food and some clothes.

Dorchester PoW camp for German soldiers. The German PoWs drew the same rations as British soldiers. The Germans treated the British in much the same way, but there was very little food for anyone in Germany by the end of the war.

German PoWs in Britain resting after working on the land.

Things to Do

1 Read Source 16.1.

   (a) What were the German prisoners working on?
   (b) In which country were they working, do you think?
   (c) How do you know they were happy?
   (d) Does the writer say he had seen them himself?
   (e) Think of as many reasons as you can why the girls were not supposed to speak or give things to the German prisoners of war.
   (f) Rewrite the paragraph from the point of view of one of the German prisoners of war.

2 Read Source 16.2.

   (a) Discuss in class all the things that make it obvious Leonard did not like the Germans.
   (b) Rewrite the paragraph from the point of view of one of the German guards.

3 The letter in Source 16.3 was written by a British student who had been visiting Germany when the war broke out.

> **Source 16.3**
>
> '*Absender*: E. R. Vincent
>   *Englanderlager Ruhleben*
> *Baracke*: XI
> *Box*: 14   2nd March 1915
> *To*: Dr Vincent   *Ort*: Hatch End
> "The Coppice", Middlesex
> *Write in pencil only Nur mit Bleistift schreiben!*
>
> Dearest Father and Mother
>   Have just received Father's PC of the 2nd and hope the cake he has sent will arrive safely. Since last writing have also received your letter of the 7th and a box of cigarettes which I enjoy exceedingly. So very, sorry to hear my dog has been bad, (food, too much or exercise insufficient, I expect). For goodness sake don't let the children give him bread, and food scraps as I'm sure he gets enough as it is. I must say that your letters and PCs come very well . . . .'
>
> From Peter Liddle, *Testimony of War 1914–18* (Michael Russell, 1979).

(a) The student and his father worked out a simple code. Write down the word in this letter before each comma. What is the message to his father?

(b) He stayed in the German prison camp for four years. Later he became one of the leading code experts in Britain in the Second World War. What is the name of the student who wrote the letter?

(c) What is the date of the letter?

(d) The camp was at Ruhleben. What barrack block was the writer in?

(e) Why do you think the Germans did not want the British to know that the prisoners were badly fed? Choose reasons from the following list. There may be more than one reason.

- The Germans were silly.
- The British would realize there was very little food in Germany for anyone, so soon Germany would give up.
- The British would be angry that British prisoners were not looked after properly.
- The British would tell the rest of the world that Germany was starving people deliberately.
- The British would rescue the prisoners by helicopter.
- The British would bomb the prison camp.
- The British would treat German prisoners badly.

(f) Discuss in class why you think the student sent this message to his father. There may be more than one reason.

(g) How do you know the German camp guards read the letters sent to Britain?

4 Compare Sources 16.1, 16.2 and 16.3. Which source do you think is the most reliable? Give reasons for your answer.

5 What do the illustrations in the chapter tell you about the lives of the prisoners?

6 What other sources would you like to see before you decided what conditions in British and German prison camps were like?

17 Food

Britain is an island. In 1914, 45 million people lived in Britain.

Staple food

The foods shown in the diagram were very important to working class people. Bread was a staple food. Richer people could afford to buy meat, butter, eggs and fresh fruit. So if ships carrying bread flour or bacon were sunk, rich people could afford to buy other food. Poor people could not.

Would Britain starve?

If Germany could stop ships reaching Britain, many British people would starve. At one time in 1917, there was only six weeks' food supply left in Britain. But before this it was obvious that something needed to be done about controlling food supplies.

These pie charts show how much of the main foods for working class people were grown in Britain and how much brought to Britain in ships.

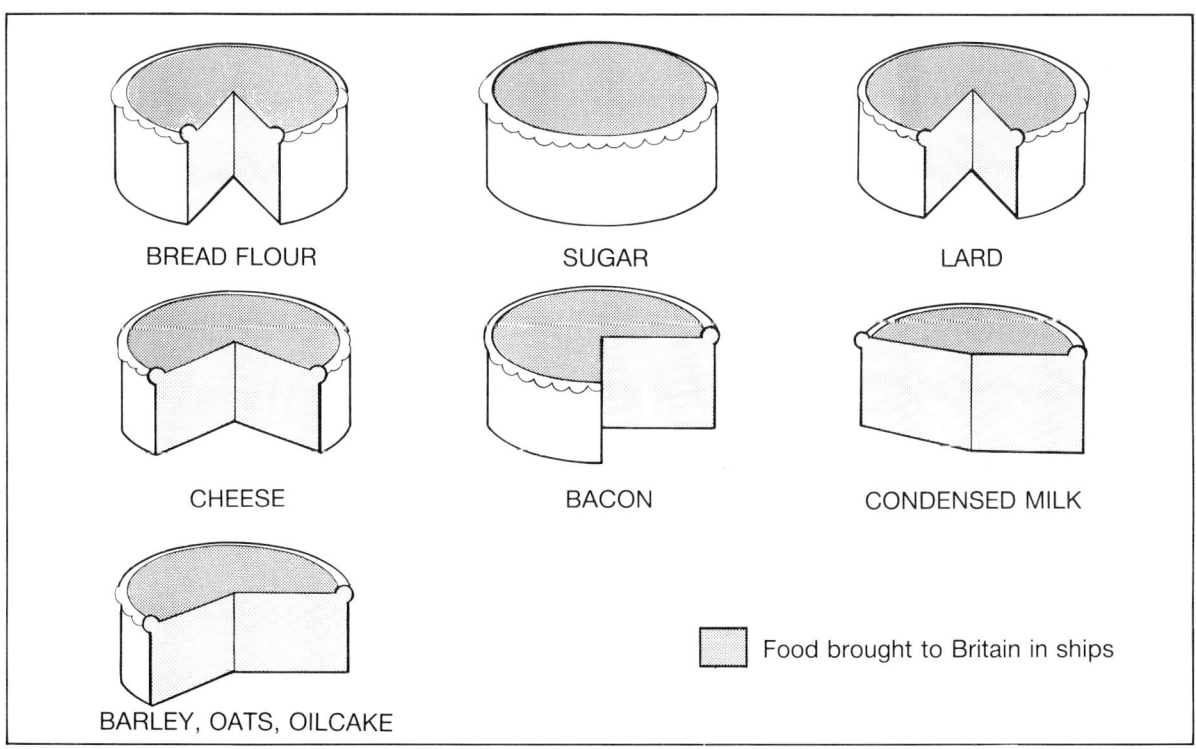

64 *The First World War 1914–18*

Eight out of ten people in Britain in 1914 were working class.

The government, 1915–16

The Liberal government decided to do something about food. The government set up five committees. The committees worked to control the supply of food in many ways. By 1916 the Liberal government had been replaced. The government was now a coalition government led by Lloyd George. He led members from different political parties. They worked together to win the war.

Ministry of Food

In December 1916 Lord Devonport visited the prime minister, Lloyd George. He said Lloyd George was 'full of enthusiasm and big ideas for food control'.

But what could be done?

The prime minister set up the Ministry of Food.

What the Ministry did

The Ministry of Food tried hard to control food supplies. It asked farmers to grow more food. Meanwhile the government started the convoy system to protect ships bringing food to Britain.

The Ministry brought in food rationing. Ordinary people were ready for rationing. They had had months of food shortages. Housewives had to queue for hours to buy food.

'Saturday 26 January 1918. Mr Lewis says the agitation among the food queues in Braintree yesterday amounted almost to a riot and the police were at their wits' end.' – Diary of Reverend Clark. Sometimes people took it more calmly!

The government did not allow official photographs of food queues to be taken during the war. Why do you think the government did not allow photos of food queues?

Food   65

Food for British soldiers piled on the quayside at Rouen in France.

Rationing

Different parts of Britain tried rationing. Then on Sunday 14 July 1918 rationing for all Britain started.

Nothing like it had been done before. Rationing meant that the government had to control food coming into Britain. It had to control food grown in Britain. The government controlled the trains and lorries that took the food to the shops. It controlled how much food went to the shops. It controlled how much food each person was allowed to have. All this was done by the Ministry of Food.

The job of rationing

British people wanted rationing. They said it was fair. It was a huge job to bring in rationing for everyone in Britain.

> *Source 17.1*
>
> ' By the middle of April 1918, after four months of work only 3,000,000 ration books out of 39,000,000 had been issued. '
>
> From Sir W. H. Beveridge, *British Food Control* (OUP, 1928).

Many women were employed in the Ministry of Food. For instance, 800 girls had jobs setting up an index of the population arranged in order of birthdays. This was such a huge job it was never finished.

Farm work

> *Source 17.2*
>
> ' We all heard we must grow more food so I went to work on a farm. I was 17 and I shared a room with three other girls. We all worked setting potatoes from 8 a.m. to 5 p.m. in heavy clay soil that had only recently been ploughed up. Lunch which we took with us was a very jolly meal and we had it in a little hut where we boiled water on a spirit kettle and made tea. I worked there doing different jobs until the end of the year. '
>
> From Gilbert Stone (ed.), *Women War Workers* (George G. Harrap, 1917).

Each ration book was issued for a number of weeks. This one shows the partly used jam, lard and meat pages. On the meat page the letters a, b and c stand for meat, d was for bacon, poultry, etc. Half a square could be handed in to the butcher for half a ration at a time (with the money to buy it as well!). Why do you think wavy patterns are printed on the coupons?

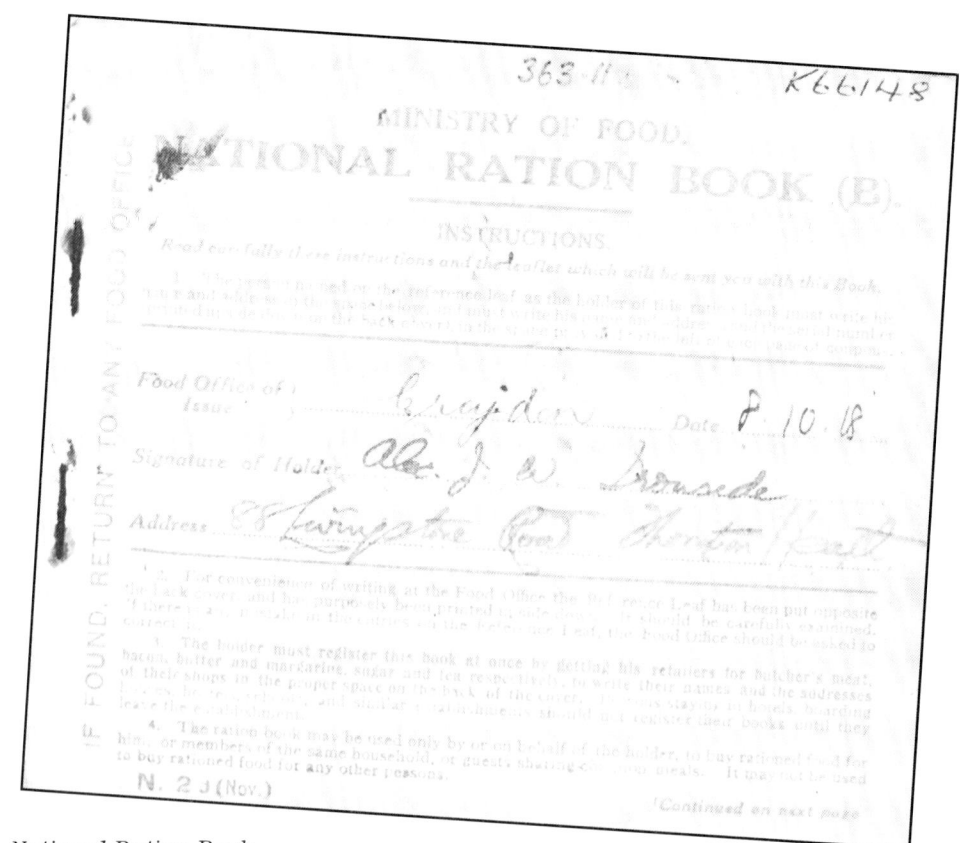

National Ration Book.

1. What is the date of this letter?
2. What is the name of the stores?
3. Who is the letter sent to?
4. Why can't the store send her a pheasant?
5. What sort of ration book did Nurse Hawthorne have? What does this tell you about her job?
6. Find out what offal is. Find out where sultanas and raisins come from. Why do you think the stores are short of sultanas and raisins?

Junior Army & Navy Stores Ltd.,
Union Street,
Aldershot.

December 2nd, 1918

Lady Hammond,
    Sherborne House,
        Camberley.

Madam,
    I am in receipt of your order of yesterday but regret that we are unable to send you a Pheasant, same being very scarce, we are, however, sending a Sheep's Head tomorrow, which I trust will be suitable. We are returning the traveller's ration book for Nurse M. Hawthorne but have not detached any coupons as Offal is now coupon free.

    Supplies of Sultanas and Raisins have not yet come to hand, but we have noted your wishes and will send a quantity at the earliest opportunity.

    I am,
        Your Ladyship's obedient servant,

            Manager, Aldershot Branch

Different ration books for different people.

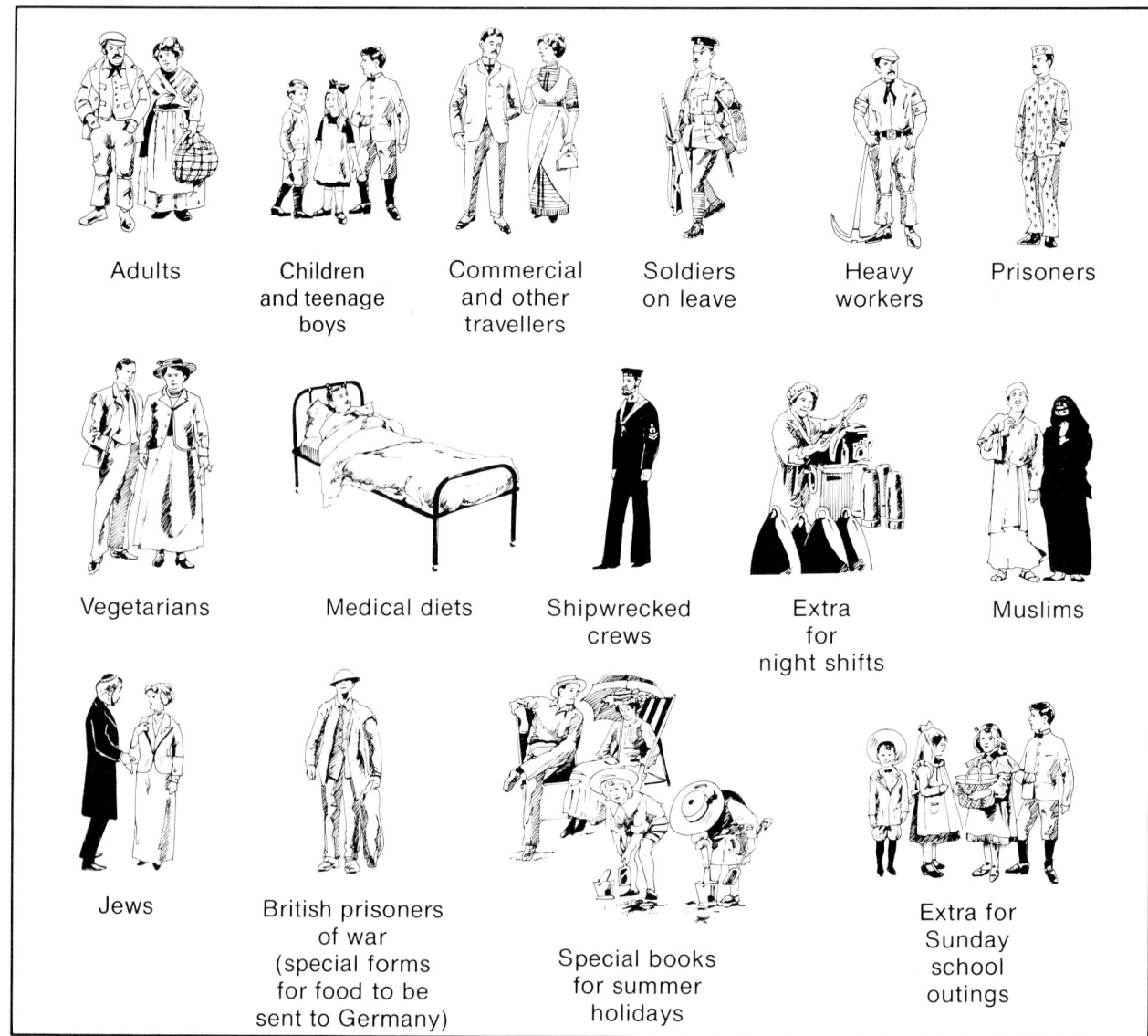

Ration books

The amount of meat you could buy with each coupon varied. With three meat coupons you could usually buy about 450 g of meat with some bone in it. Meat coupons had to be handed in for meat meals in a restaurant.

Other rations are set out in Source 17.3. The amount varied with the time of year and the shipping losses. The one in Source 17.3 is for an adult in one week.

Source 17.3

Jam and marmalade	113 g
Tea	56 g
Bacon and ham	340 g
Lard	56 g
Butter and margarine	113 g
Sugar	226 g

Things to Do

1 Look at the diagrams on pages 63 and 64 and read the section headed 'Staple food'.

   (a) Write out the following paragraph choosing the correct word from the brackets.

   In 1914 the (minority/majority) of people in Britain were working class. Bread was a (staple/stable) food for working class people. Staple food means that you (never eat it/eat it most of the time/sometimes eat it). (Most/half/some) of the bread and lard was imported. It was imported into Britain in (trains/space ships/aeroplanes/ships/cars).

   (b) Look at the diagram on page 63. Why do you think British meat might have become scarce?

2 (a) Keep a record of the food you eat in one week. (To be accurate you must weigh all the portions.) Compare your amounts to those shown in Source 17.3, plus the meat ration mentioned in the section headed 'Ration books'.

   (b) What difficulties did you have in comparing the amounts of sugar and fats? What does this tell you about food preparation now and then?

   (c) What foods are not mentioned that you eat regularly? Why do you think this is? There could be several reasons.

18 Getting Better

Wounded soldiers needed rest. They needed time to get better. Many got better. They went back to fight again.

Sometimes hotels were used as convalescent homes. Often wealthy people opened their country houses. They took in wounded soldiers as house guests. Usually the wounded soldiers who went to country houses were officers.

> *Source 18.1*
>
> 'Nutwood Manor was everything a wounded officer could wish for. Leaning my elbows on the window sill I gazed down at the yew hedges of a formal garden, woods and meadows and far away stood the Sussex Downs. Often during the next few weeks I was able to forget about the war.'
>
> From Siegfried Sassoon, *Memoirs of an Infantry Officer* (Faber & Faber, 1930).

Ordinary soldiers got better at home or in special convalescent homes.

Treatment

New treatments were tried out to help men recover. Sometimes treatment could take a long time.

> *Source 18.2*
>
> 'At that time Edward had just begun his period of sick leave. A serious injury to the nerves of his arm caused him intense pain for months, and he had a course of massage which lasted for nearly a year.'
>
> From Vera Brittain, *Testament of Youth* (Victor Gollancz, 1933).

A sign early in the war outside a London hospital.

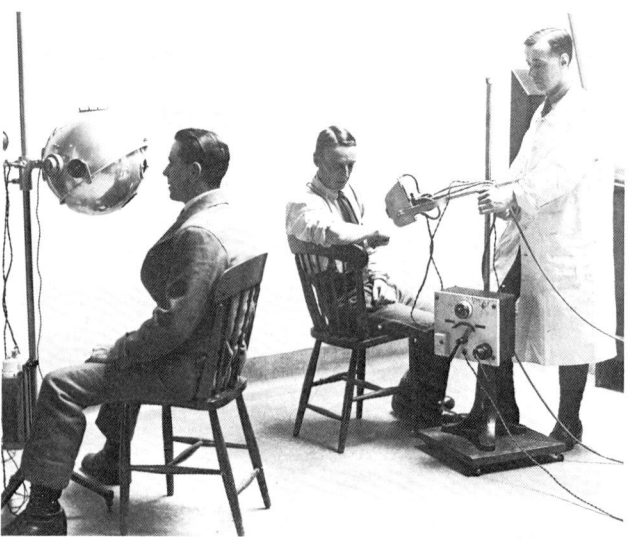

New ultra ray treatment at a London hospital.

Invalided out

Some soldiers were very badly wounded. They were invalided out of the army.

> *Source 18.3*
>
> ❛I'm fed up to the teeth with wandering around in mufti [civilian clothes] and getting black looks from people who pass remarks to the effect that it's about time I joined up. Meanwhile I exist on my provisional pension (3s [15p] a day). A few days touring round these munition areas would give you food for thought. The average conversation is about the high cost of beer and how to evade military service by bluffing the tribunals.❜
>
> Letter from Birdie Mansfield in Yorkshire to Siegfried Sassoon. From Siegfried Sassoon, *Memoirs of an Infantry Officer* (Faber & Faber, 1930).

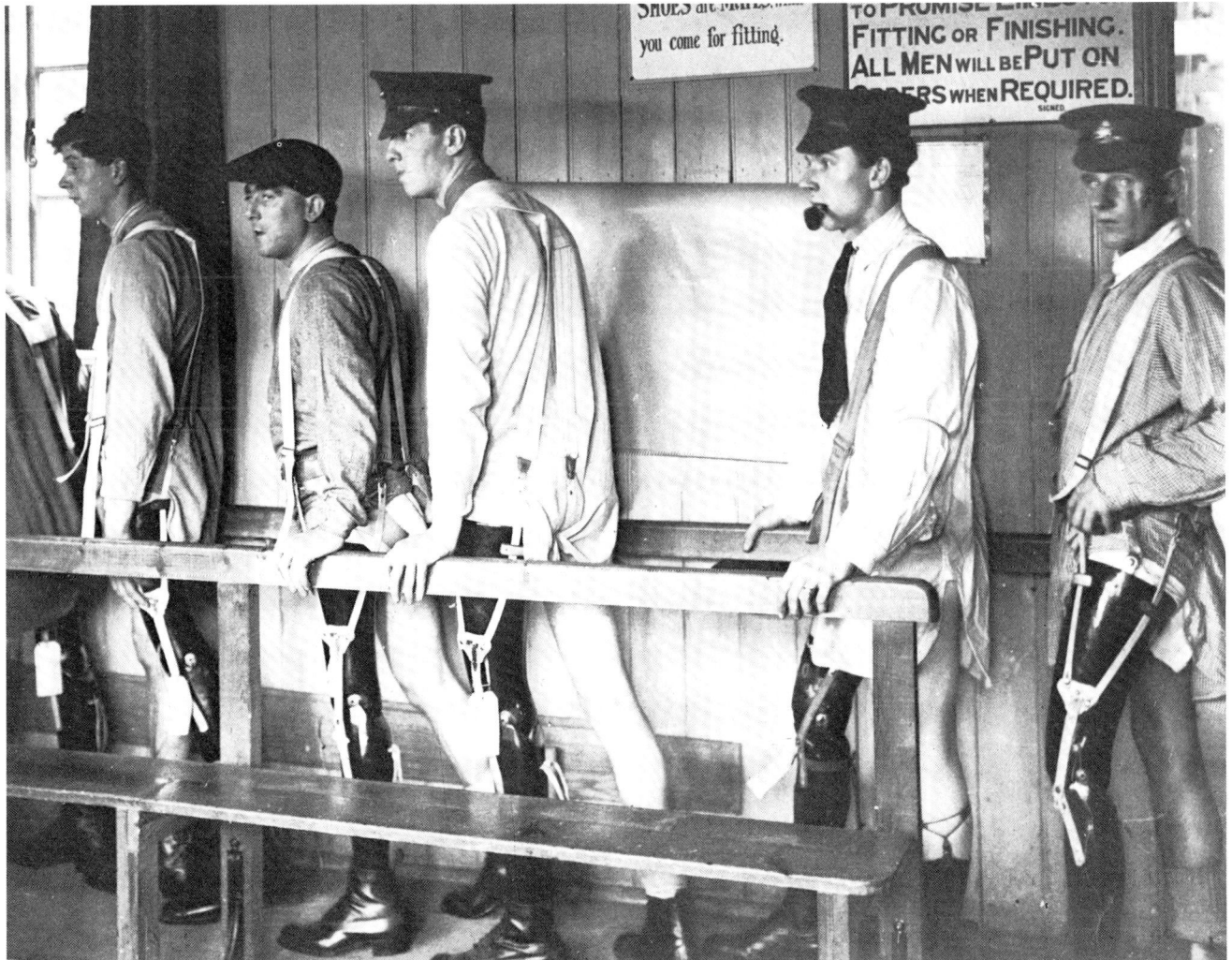

Legs were made of wood in large workshops. Aluminium had been tried before the war, but was not generally used.

72 The First World War 1914–18

Women footballers and wounded at a Red Cross fête in Malvern in 1918.

A poster for convalescents.

Things to Do

1 Read Source 18.3.

  (a) Who was the letter from?

  (b) Why did people give the writer black looks?

  (c) Did the writer think the black looks were fair or unfair?

  (d) What are munitions?

  (e) What was a tribunal?

  (f) What do you think a provisional pension was?

  (g) Why was beer expensive in the First World War?

  (h) How do you know that the writer and the man he was writing to were soldiers? Find as many reasons as you can.

2 Look at Sources 18.1 and 18.3. What makes you think that both soldiers felt they lived in a different world from civilians?

19 Life at Home

The war started with excitement and cheering. It would be glorious. It would be over by Christmas 1914. But it was not.

Cost of the war

Britain lost many men in the war. So did countries in the British empire. The war also cost a great deal of money. The government raised the money in taxes and by getting people to lend money to support the war. This was very patriotic.

Government control

In 1916 the Liberal government thought that people should be able to choose whether to fight or not. But the war was so big. It became impossible for the Liberal government to let people do as they liked. So a new coalition government came to power. It promised to fight the war. A law was passed in Parliament. Every fit man *had* to fight.

Other government control

The government started to control the making of munitions. The government took more interest in the health of children (future soldiers) and women (essential as mothers and workers). Slowly people accepted more government control.

Slowly people realized the war affected everyone in Britain.

CARRYING ON.

What nationality is the man firing the gun? Who is he firing at? Which country do you think the man is running away from? What is the artist saying about the war? Think carefully and find as many things as you can.

Food control

Much of Britain's food came from other countries. People queued for food. The government decided to ration food. Magazines published wartime recipes. Cookery classes were held.

74 *The First World War 1914–18*

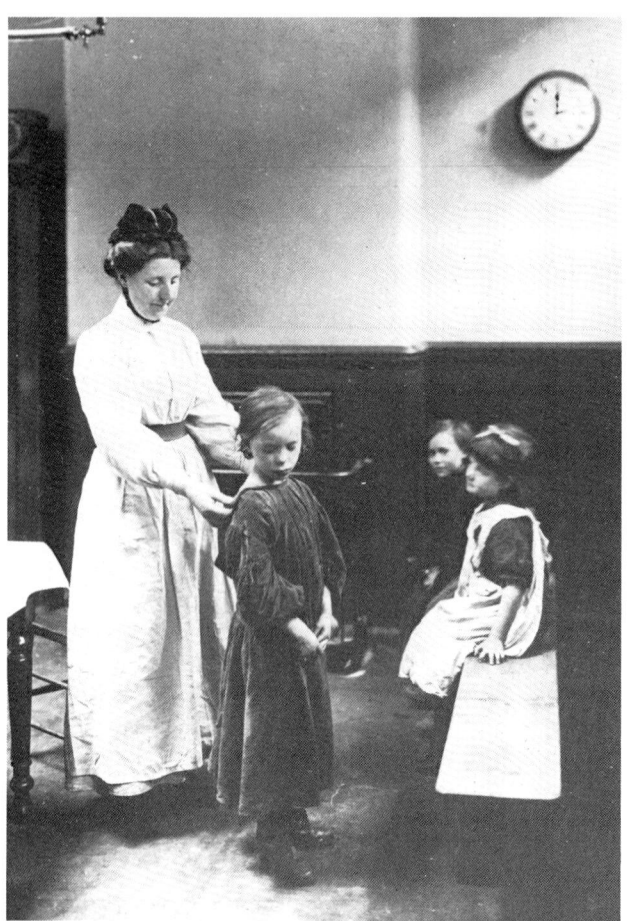

Free medical attention for school children began just before the war. Care for families grew during the war, with the opening of welfare clinics.

Land girls in training, 1918.

Jobs to be done

Rich people found it difficult to get servants. Mrs Masefield, the wife of the poet John Masefield, suddenly learnt 'the ways of hens and ducks' and had to send her husband off to do the shopping.

Young people did many different jobs. Women who loved to organize committees, run hospitals, raise money for the war and so on, did a lot to help the war effort.

Training camps

Many soldiers meant the need for many training camps in Britain. There were soldiers in Britain from all over the empire. The United States of America came into the war in 1917. Many American soldiers came to Britain.

Bombing

Never before had death dropped from the sky. By the end of 1915 people were getting used to bombs.

Source 19.1

'The night we came up to London there was a zeppelin raid. I was at Isabel's when suddenly "bang" went the guns. In an instant I was in the street running with head down to get home to the children. The sky was lit up with searchlights and bright bursts from the shells but the enemy was four miles away at least, in the Strand.

When I got in John was calmly writing a shopping list. He is more used to the bombs. He was not going to bother about them as he couldn't do anything. So I filled the bath and turned off the gas and by that time the sounds were distancing. The children slept through it all.'

Mrs Masefield. From C. B. Smith, *John Masefield: A Life* (OUP, 1978).

Life at Home 75

Punch *cartoon about the craze for knitting for soldiers.*

Girl guides collecting waste paper. The paper was sold to help run the girl guides' laundry which did all the laundry for the local Red Cross hospital.

A free buffet (run by volunteers) for soldiers at Victoria Station.

Indian soldiers at an army camp in the New Forest in the south of England. There were army camps all over Britain.

Things to Do

1. What was a zeppelin?
2. Was it safer in a house or in the street, do you think?
3. Which was the safest part of a house if bombs were falling?
4. Why did Mrs Masefield fill the bath?
5. Why did she turn off the gas?
6. Find the words in the word square. All the words in it are listed below.

Parliament	law	hens
patriotic	recipes	queue
war	bomb	rich
training camp	gas	slept
taxes	zeppelin	list
end	fit	America
men	sky	all
power	lit	miles
empire	food	women

```
P A R L I A M E N T O
0 A Z E B L S H A R G
W R T Y C L L X C A A
A R S R K I E T S I L
M E N N I S P X F N R
E W D N E O T E I I H
R O S L Q H T L S N T
I P I D T N E I X G I
C M 0 A E P U T C C O
A O E M P I R E W A L
F D O E W A R B O M B
A W Z Q U E U E X P Q
```

20 A Woman's Magazine

Woman's Weekly is a best selling magazine today. The magazine started in 1911. It was very popular during the First World War.

Women's magazines are important. They spread new ideas. They also reflect what many ordinary women are thinking and doing.

Source 20.1

By 1917 most stories in the magazine had a war background and a hero in uniform. (The young man died but his tall handsome soldier brother, Ted, fell in love with Nell.)

78   The First World War 1914–18

Source 20.2

What is the date of this double page? About how much of the double page is concerned with the war (all/half/more than a quarter/a quarter)? Do you think milkless tea was the greatest of the soldiers' worries in France?

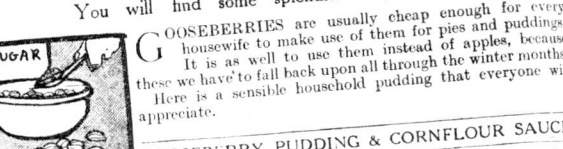

WOMAN'S WEEKLY

ACTRESS TELLS SECRET.

A Well-known Actress Tells How She Darkened Her Grey Hair and Promoted Its Growth with a Simple Home-made mixture.

Miss Blanche Rose, a well-known actress, who darkened her grey hair with a simple preparation which she mixed at home, in a recent interview, made the following statement: "Any lady or gentleman can darken their grey hair and make it soft and glossy with this simple recipe, which they can mix at home. To a half-pint of water add 1 oz. of bay rum, a small box of Orlex Compound, and ¼ oz. of glycerine. These ingredients can be bought at any chemist's at very little cost. Apply to the hair twice a week until it becomes the required shade. This will make a grey-haired person look 20 years younger. It is also fine to promote the growth of hair, relieves itching and scalp humours, and is excellent for dandruff and falling hair."—(ADVT.)

FOR BEAUTY AND DURABILITY

No Dyes can compare with

MAYPOLE (Soap) DYES

Colours, 4d. Black, 6d.

Send for the Free Booklet, "The Perfection of Home Dyeing," and Amusing Novelties for Children to (Dept. R7),

MAYPOLE COMPANY (1899), Ltd.,
17, Cumming St., King's Cross, N.

Oatine

clears the skin by thoroughly cleansing the pores, removing the dirt that soap and water cannot and cannot reach. It is the secret of beauty.

A FREE SAMPLE

of OATINE CREAM will be sent on application, or for 3d. in stamps, a box containing five of the Oatine preparations.

THE OATINE CO.,
258, Oatine Bldgs., Boro', London, S.E.

GRAVES of Sheffield

FOR EVERYTHING
ON EASY MONTHLY TERMS.
Write for Suit, Costume, or Raincoat Patterns, or Catalogue of Cycles, Gramophones and Records, Furniture, Sheffield Cutlery, Boots and Shoes, Watches & Jewellery, Linoleums etc.
J. G. GRAVES, LTD., SHEFFIELD.

When communicating with Advertisers please mention "Woman's Weekly."

TESTED RECIPES.

GOOSEBERRY DISHES.

The gooseberry is a delicious fruit. Make the most of it while you have the opportunity. You will find some splendid recipes here.

GOOSEBERRIES are usually cheap enough for every housewife to make use of them for pies and puddings. It is as well to use them instead of apples, because these we have to fall back upon all through the winter months. Here is a sensible household pudding that everyone will appreciate.

GOOSEBERRY PUDDING & CORNFLOUR SAUCE.

MAKE a suet crust by mixing together half a pound of flour, four ounces of finely shredded suet, one teaspoonful of baking-powder, a little salt, and about a gill of water to form a paste.

Turn this on to a floured board, and roll it out to the size of a basin, leaving sufficient for the top.

Line the basin carefully, leaving no spaces; then put in enough of the washed and prepared gooseberries to half fill the basin. Add two tablespoonfuls of brown sugar, and then the remainder of the fruit. A very little water should be added.

Cover the top closely with the remaining suet crust, pressing the edges well together, or the juice will ooze out in the cooking and spoil the appearance of the dish altogether.

Tie the pudding up firmly, and either boil or steam it for not less than two hours.

Gooseberries, especially young ones, are very sour, but a cornflour sauce will take off this sharpness and greatly improve the pudding.

DELICIOUS GOOSEBERRY FOOL.

THERE are so many ways of making this, but none better than the following:

Take two pounds of gooseberries, half a pound of sugar, one gill of water, and half a pint of custard.

Boil the water and sugar together for five minutes, then put in the gooseberries, already washed and picked. Cook the fruit until it is quite tender, then rub the fruit through a sieve or strainer. Mix it with the custard, and serve cold in a glass dish.

Egg-powder can quite well be used for the custard here. The flavour of the fruit is so pronounced that the actual taste of the custard will not be noticed.

STEAMED BATTER AND GOOSEBERRY SAUCE.

HAVE you ever tried this? It is very nourishing and nice.
Make the batter by mixing together six ounces of flour and a quarter of a teaspoonful of salt. Make a hole in the centre, and stir in two yolks of eggs. Add half a pint of milk gradually, and mix it to a batter. Heat it for ten minutes, and then add half a pint of water. Let the batter stand for a short time. Meanwhile whisk up the whites stiffly, and stir them quickly into the batter with one ounce of castor sugar. Steam the mixture in a well-buttered tin for two hours, and serve it with this sauce:

A COMPANY TRIFLE.

A GOOSEBERRY trifle is very delightful, and is most inexpensive too. If you have any left over plain cake—preferably sponge—crumble it up into a pretty glass dish. A few small macaroon biscuits will improve the trifle still further.

Stew a pound of gooseberries until they are nicely tender, sieve them, and pour them over the sponge. Leave this until it is cool, and then pour over it a good cornflour custard. Decorate the top with blanched almonds and a little whipped cream if there is any at hand.

If you have not quite sufficient fruit for a trifle, sieve what there is, and add to it some very fine breadcrumbs to make up the required quantity.

Whether you are making a pudding or a pie, always add the sugar half way and then fill up the dish, otherwise the sugar is apt to affect the crust as well as sweetening the fruit unevenly.

Never use an iron spoon when dealing with fruit, the acid will act upon the metal and cause the fruit to taste very unpleasant. A whole dish is sometimes spoilt from this cause.

When fruit is sieved in this way, the strained liquid is called a puree. The gooseberries must be pressed through the sieve with a wooden spoon.

The quickest way of working is to rub with the back of the bowl of the spoon with your fingers in the bowl of it and on the handle.

Sieves need very careful cleaning. After scrubbing and scraping they should be well dried and hung in the open air until they are perfectly dry.

Some people like to crumble the cake, soak it in sherry or fruit juice and then beat it up with a fork before putting it into the dish—this is for either a fruit or an ordinary trifle. Biscuits of any plain variety can be added if there is not enough cake.

Remember that gooseberries need a great deal of sugar—taste them always when they are cooked for a trifle or any such dish.

April 17, 1915

MADE FROM THREE HANDKERCHIEFS.

A NOVEL CUSHION COVER.

FINE embroidered handkerchiefs are simply splendid for fancy-work. They may be used for all kinds of things, and are specially suitable for ra.ing bags, cushions, and camisoles.

Here is quite a new idea for a cushion cover, and one which I am sure will be appreciated by the girl who loves making dainty things for the home. It is made out of fine lawn embroidered handkerchiefs with Valenciennes insertion. Besides being very easy to make, it is quite inexpensive, and looks very dainty over a foundation of blue or pink silk. It is also very effective when used over black or Royal-blue satin.

To make the cover you will require two handkerchiefs about twelve inches square, and one handkerchief six inches square, and two yards of fine Valenciennes, about an inch and a half wide.

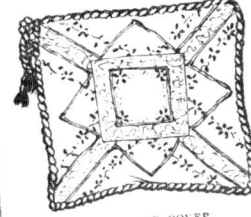

THE FINISHED COVER.

The smallest handkerchief is first edged all round with the insertion, care being taken that the corners are neatly mitred.

The two larger handkerchiefs are now cut diagonally across from corner to corner, thus giving four pieces. On each of these pieces, the point formed by the uncut corner is turned back sufficiently to form a triangular flap, measuring six inches at the base. These four pieces are now joined with insertion, as shown in the sketch. When joined they form a square, with an opening in the centre, into which your small handkerchief, already edged with insertion, will be found to fit. Set the small handkerchief in this opening and neatly sew it into place, with small oversewing stitches.

The back of the cushion cover is made of lawn, which must match your handkerchiefs as nearly as possible. One end of the cover is left open, having one side finished off with a flap, and the other side with a false hem. On the flap are sewn small linen buttons, and on the hem buttonholes to correspond are worked. This makes it very easy to remove the cover in order to launder it when it is soiled.

THE CALL TO BRITAIN

I'm doing *my* bit, save me from milkless tea.

Send some tins of

NESTLÉ'S MILK

to your Soldier Friend

He needs milk more than anything

"*Milk is our greatest luxury.*"—Soldier's letter.

If you want to save our soldiers from Milkless Tea, write us, with your Grocer's name and address, for a subscription card for Tins of Nestlé's Milk—Nestlé's, B.E.F. Dept., 6 Eastcheap, London, E.C.

Peach's Curtains

GUIDE BOOK FREE.
DIRECT FROM LOOMS AND ACTUAL MAKERS.
Every kind of Curtain Material.
LACE CURTAINS, IMPERIAL HEM CURTAINS, NETS MUSLINS, CASEMENT FABRICS, LINENS, LACES, BLOUSES

ORIGINAL "POPULAR" SELECTION, 21/-. Carriage Paid.
No. 1 9 contains **5 pairs** excellent quality Curtains, Carriage Paid. White or Ecru, as follows:— 2 pairs alive. Old Lace Design Curtains for Dining Room, 3½ yds. by 60 ins. 1 pair, charming Border, Festoon Centre, 3 yds by 2 yds. 2 pairs Fancy Drawing Room Curtains, 3 yds by 45 ins. **The highest value obtainable.**
Net Bedroom Curtains, 3 yds by 45 ins. **6.11** pair. | Greek Key Muslin Curtains, 3 yds. **7/3** pair
"Chesterfield" Lace Curtains, 3 yds., **9/-** pair. | Hemstitched Muslin, 48 in. wide, **11d.** yard.
"Sweet Pea" Imperial Hem do., 3 yds., **11/6** pair. | "Sunfast" Cyprus Casement Cloth, **8½d.** yard.
"Wisteria" Imperial Hem do., 3 yds., **11/6** pair. |
The above and many others are fully illustrated in the List.
SEND NOW for BEST BOOK FOR CURTAINS. **It WILL SAVE YOU MONEY.**
S. PEACH & SONS, 159, The Looms, NOTTINGHAM.

WHEN A MAN KNOWS BEST.
By MRS. MARRYAT.

Care of "Woman's Weekly,"
The Fleetway House,
Farringdon Street,
London, E.C.

MY DEAR FRIENDS,—What would YOUR verdict be in a case such as this, of which I heard the other day? A soldier is crippled for life. He wants to break off his engagement.

The girl's parents quite agree to this. They think his view is right. The girl thinks otherwise. She says "No." She wishes to marry him in spite of his permanent disablement, and does not wish the engagement to be broken off. IS SHE RIGHT?

Sentimentalists will cry offhand: "Of course she is!" But there is another side to be considered—namely, the view taken by the man himself. No one knows his feelings so well as he knows them. He knows what he has to bear. He feels matrimony is not for him. It may be kinder to let him be free. His own burden is sufficient for him to bear. There are some burdens one can best bear alone. This is probably one of them. The girl should not add to it by insisting upon sacrificing herself. It is sometimes forgotten that many men shrink from being the object of a life-long sacrifice on a girl's part. They could not endure to accept the gift, and feel they had allowed a girl to tie herself for the rest of her life to a man who could do little to make her happy and comfortable, who might indeed be obliged to demand from her unceasing care and nursing.

Some men glory in the thought that a woman is willing to renounce everything for their sakes. To others this would be a positively poisonous thought. Life would be unbearable to them if they thought the girl they loved had become a martyr for their sakes. Who is to say which of these classes of men is right? For me, I think they are both right, according to their lights and their temperaments. To oblige a man to marry when he feels the sacrifice of the girl is more than he can bear would be cruelty, not kindness, and the girl who realises this will, if she really loves him, let him have his own way.

Your friend,
MARY MARRYAT.

ANSWERS TO QUESTIONS.

TRAINING AS NURSE.
K. T. (Clapham).—To be a "trained" nurse you must spend three years in a general hospital as a "probationer." Then you must pass an examination, and obtain a certificate to prove that you have been trained and have satisfactorily passed the exam. The duties of a probationer are to attend on the patients in the hospital under the supervision of the staff nurses, the "sisters," and the matron, also to assist in keeping the wards tidy, dusting them, etc.

TABLE MANNERS.
M. W.—A lady can help her guests to vegetables if there is no maid to hand the dishes, or the guests can pass the dish round. Each one who is served with pudding should begin to eat it. There is no need to wait to begin until all are served.

ON THE LAND.
Seeing my brothers and friends joining the colours I feel I must do something for my dear old country. I would very much like to go on the land. If you think this is suitable can you tell me what to do?—"PATRIOT."

YOU can't do better than go on the land. It is the most patriotic work women can do at present. Apply to the Women's National Land Service Corps, 50, Upper Baker Street, London, N.W. They are asking for strong young women as recruits for farm work. You should also apply to your nearest Labour Exchange.

"VERY ANXIOUS."—You can't marry your uncle by marriage!

TO BRIGHTEN DULL HAIR.
EMILY A. S.—Wash your hair once a month with quillaia bark. You can get this quite cheaply from a chemist. Ask for it in sticks, not in powder. Take a piece as long as your finger, shake it about in a basin of hot water till a good lather results. Wash in this, and rinse in tepid water. It will make your hair soft and bright.

A QUESTION OF PRESENTS.
I have been keeping company with a young man for about six months. His birthday comes first. Would it be correct for me to give him a small present? I find your paper most useful.—"DORA."

GIVE him a buttonhole for his coat. It would be unwise to give anything more valuable than that. I am so glad you find the paper useful.

TO CURE PSORIASIS.
"MOLLIE."—The reader who says she has a cure for psoriasis has not communicated it. I wish she would. I will keep your address, and let you know if I hear.

TO CLEAR THE COMPLEXION.
"POPPY."—Too much sweetstuff of any kind is not good for the complexion. Tomatoes have much the same uses as other vegetables and fruits. In moderation they are good for the blood.

"POPPY."—A girl of nineteen—or any other age—should walk every day as far as she finds time for without tiring herself very much. Walks that exhaust the strength are not good at any age.

"LAMBKIN."—Has the curate asked you to go out with him? Everything depends on that.

"PERPLEXED MAY."—It is always a very risky thing for a girl to make the acquaintance of a man to whom she has not been introduced.

PROBATIONER IN A CHILDREN'S HOSPITAL.
Could you tell me at what age one is allowed to enter a children's hospital as a probationer?—"A LONELY GIRL."

GENERALLY at about twenty. I advise you to get "How to Become a Nurse," by Sir H. Burdett. It will give you all the information you require, also the names, addresses, and particulars of nurses' salaries, etc., of every hospital in the United Kingdom.

RETURNING THE ENGAGEMENT RING.
"ANXIOUS."—No one can compel you to return the ring your former sweetheart gave you. I am afraid I must say you are well rid of him. A man who, after having gone out with you for five years, can then demand the return of the ring, with threats of "further trouble" if you don't give it up, is too contemptible for words. He would not make a good husband, and you will be very foolish to break your heart about the business.

"VIOLET."—I can't advise on such a subject here. Why not have sent an addressed envelope for reply by post?

WRITE TO MRS. MARRYAT.
Everyone is to feel at home on Mrs. Marryat's page. Father's, mothers, daughters, sons, each and all are welcome. This is a woman's paper, but very often we have letters from the menfolk, and right gladly we welcome them.

If you want advice on any subject, let Mrs. Marryat help you. Write to her, care of "Woman's Weekly," The Fleetway House, Farringdon Street, E.C. Should you have a question to ask, that needs a prompt answer, send along a stamped addressed envelope, and Mrs. Marryat will reply through the post. Otherwise, look for your answer on this page, though not in the next issue.

"PUSS."—You can buy pumice-stone at any chemist's for a penny or two per piece. Thanks a thousand times for your kind wishes and compliments. It is most nourishing to my vanity to read that you think I am "splendid."

TAKE BABY TO THE DOCTOR.
S. R. P.—I always advise mothers whose babies come out in a rash to show the child to a doctor, because sometimes a rash may be a symptom of one of the infectious illnesses, or it may be due to some constitutional disease which urgently requires medical treatment. This is one of the cases in which it is better—ever so much better—to be sure than sorry.

"PANSY LEAF."—Why not have both girls for friends, as you say one did you a good turn once? Perhaps you are making too much of her "falseness." There is good in everyone. Try to find her good points.

HAIR IN CURL AT SEASIDE.
"ELEANOR."—Try the recipe kindly sent by a reader for a lotion that will keep the hair waved for a considerable time. I have given it before, but give it here again for your benefit, as you want something to keep your hair in curl at the seaside. Readers have written to say they have found the effect excellent. Half an ounce of quince-seeds boiled in half a pint of water till it is like gum. Keep in a corked bottle. Add a few drops of spirits or eau-de-Cologne to make it keep. Damp the hair with this at bedtime, plait tightly, or roll up firmly. When combed out in the morning, the hair will be beautifully wavy. A chemist can get the quince-seeds for you, 4d. for half an ounce. I am told it is just the thing for hair at the seaside.

KID BOOTS FOR TENDER FEET.
NELLIE H. T.—What I think you need are boots made of kid. Leather is often too hard and stiff for tender feet. I would recommend you to have a consultation with a good bootmaker. He could explain why your boots get too large after being too tight and hurting at first. I believe the trouble lies with the leather. Don't wear it; wear soft kid instead.

SENDING CIGARETTES.
"TIMID NELL."—You don't say how long you have known the young man, or on what terms you and he are, so I can't advise as to sending him cigarettes.

TOO THIN.
"WORRIED MAUD."—Here is a short recipe by which to get fat: *Eat and rest.* As to your shoulder-blade, which is further out than the other, I would advise you to let a surgeon see it. No one who has not examined it could tell you how it should be treated.

"ANXIOUS INQUIRER."—I am sorry to say that there is no treatment by which thick ankles can be quickly reduced. Try wearing boots for a time.

TO WHITEN THE NECK.
F. M. H.—Use vanishing cream, or else this cheap and simple method. Rub a little pure, clean grease into the skin—just a little, so that the skin shall not be actually oily—then dust over this with fuller's-earth or violet-powder. Lemon-juice and rose-water will bleach the skin.

DOCTOR'S ACCOUNT.
Could you please tell me if one can demand particulars and dates of a doctor's account? I have recently paid one, but no particulars as to medicine and attendance were given.—"BOBS."

I SUPPOSE you *could* demand particulars, but it would make unpleasantness with the doctor, as doctors never do furnish these items when sending in their accounts. These are not the same things as bills from a shop for goods supplied. People often forget this fact.

A Woman's Magazine 81

Source 20.3

The problems page in Woman's Weekly, *August 1918.*

1 Read the sections headed

- A QUESTION OF PRESENTS
- PERPLEXED MAY
- RETURNING THE ENGAGEMENT RING
- SENDING CIGARETTES

(a) Which problems sound different from problems today?
(b) Which problems are the same?
(c) What does this tell you about the role of women in society in 1918?

2 Read the sections headed

- TO BRIGHTEN DULL HAIR
- HAIR IN A CURL AT SEASIDE

Choose one of these problems. Write briefly the advice that you would give today. Why couldn't that advice be given in 1918?

3 Read the letter written by Mary Marryat at the top of the first column. Do you agree with her advice not to marry the man? Give reasons for your answer.

4 Do you think that society in Britain in 1918 was

(a) dominated by women?
(b) a partnership between men and women?
(c) dominated by men?

Look for evidence in the problem page to support your view. Then find some more evidence in this book to back your answer.

Source 20.4

A soldier receiving his Christmas parcel. This drawing of life in the trenches appeared in Woman's Weekly, *in November 1917. How does it compare with photographs you have seen and accounts you have read of soldiers in the trenches? Why has the artist drawn it like this?*

In 1917 the Russian Revolution started. People in Britain were worried. What was happening? Was the Tsar (emperor) of Russia safe? What would happen if Russia (Britain's ally) stopped fighting the Germans? Everyone was talking and thinking about Russia. Try doing this puzzle which appeared in Woman's Weekly *in September 1917.*

Source 20.5

82 *The First World War 1914–18*

Source 20.6

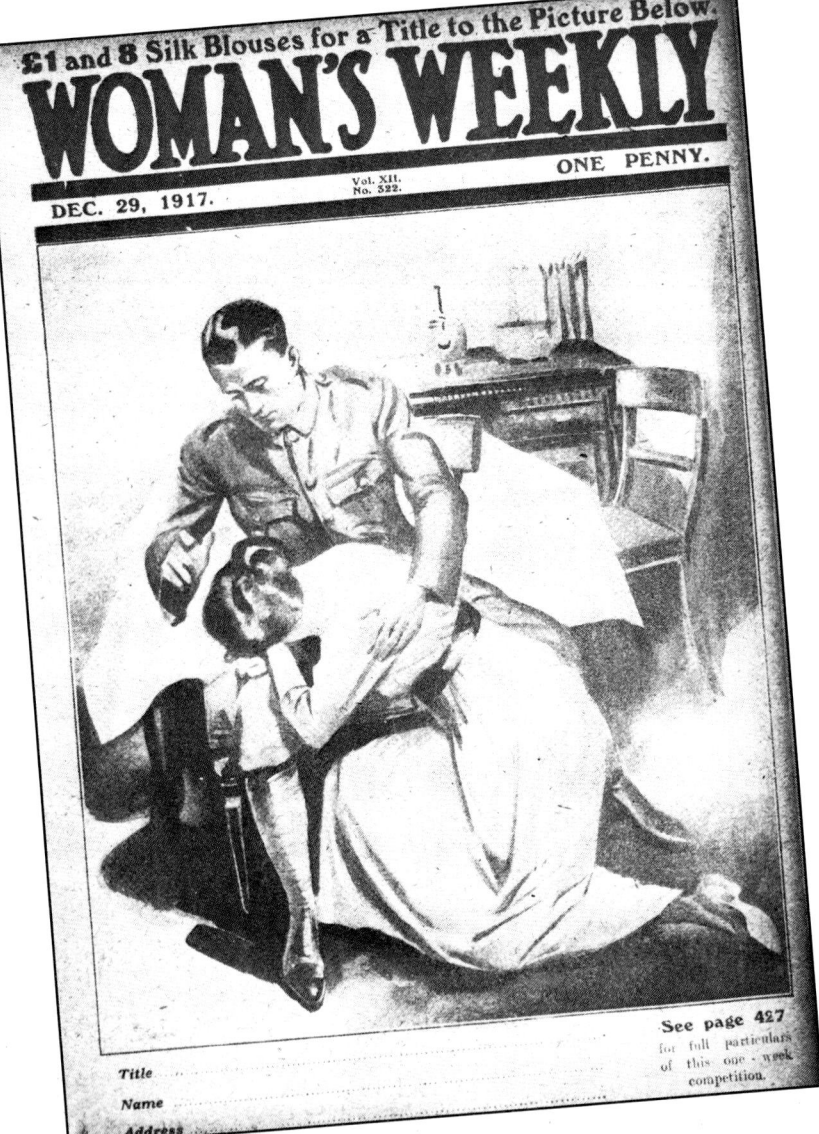

What date is the cover of the magazine? Thinking back to all you have seen and read on the First World War, write down a title to this picture.

Things to Do

Design your own cover for *Woman's Weekly* in the First World War. Look back carefully in this chapter to see what sort of audience the magazine is aimed at and what topics are written about. Also bear in mind women's war work.

21 The End of the War

On 11 November 1918 the Germans and their allies gave up fighting. The war was over.

> *Source 21.1*
>
> ‛ The crowd in the streets is tremendous. People are wandering in groups, wearing flags or ribbons. Sailors are going down the street arm-in-arm in long rows. Tin whistles and bands and church bells ringing.
>
> In the hospital they are sitting up in bed singing and some of the influenza patients are dancing on the floor.
>
> In the women's wards there's only one remark: "Ma man will be home soon noo". ’
>
> Dr Mildred Clark in a letter to her father the Reverend A. Clark. From Reverend A. Clark, *Echoes of the Great War* (OUP, 1985).

Vera Brittain

Vera Brittain realized that the young men she had grown up with were all dead.

> *Source 21.2*
>
> ‛ Already this was a different world from the one that I had known during four life-long years. And in that brightly lit world I should have no part. ’
>
> From Vera Brittain, *Testament of Youth* (Victor Gollancz, 1933).

Survivors

Mrs Webster's husband had been gassed. She nursed him for fifteen years. Harry Pattenden was badly wounded in the legs. He never played cricket again. John Goods came home fit and well and died in the influenza epidemic that swept the world just after the war.

Victory march in London, 19 July 1919. Indian soldiers passing up the Mall.

Two officers with a barrel organ in London in 1920.

War memorials

Many towns and villages built war memorials. They did not want to forget the men who had died.

The future

People had fought to defeat Germany. They had fought for a better world after the war. They had fought for better homes. They had fought for a better life for their children. These were things that people felt they were fighting for.

The Germans and their allies had fought for what they believed in too. Now Europe had to settle down. It was not going to be easy. It was one thing to win the war. It was another thing to make the peace last.

The unknown warrior

One unknown soldier was buried in Westminster Abbey. He represented all the soldiers who had died in the war. A newspaper journalist watched the procession as the coffin was carried down Whitehall.

> **Source 21.3**
>
> 'What have we the living to say to the dead who pass by in shadowy hosts? They died for no mean thing. They died that the world might be a better and cleaner place for those who lived and for those who come after. As that unknown soldier is borne down Whitehall he will issue a silent challenge to the living world to say whether it was worthy of his sacrifice. And if we are honest with ourselves we shall not find the answer easy.'
>
> From Alpha of the Plough, *Many Furrows* (J.M. Dent, 1924).

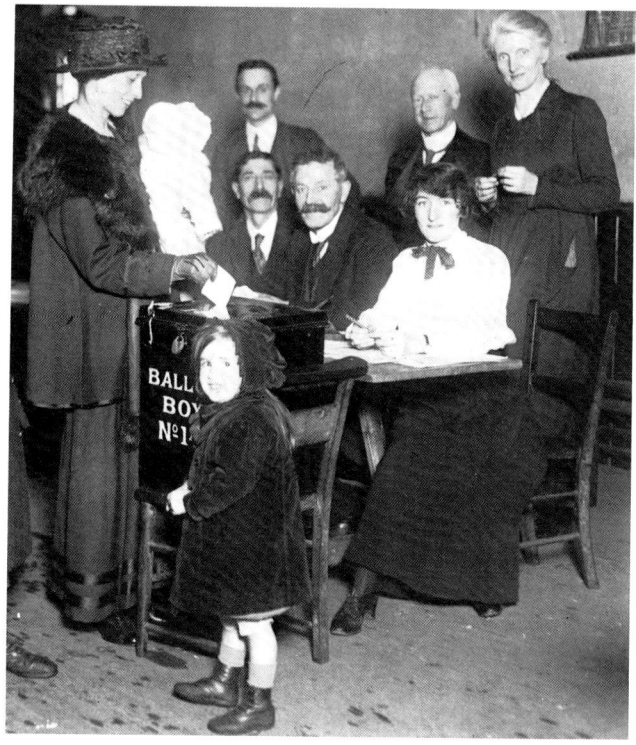

Election scene in December 1918.

An all-electric kitchen. How many gadgets in the kitchen use electricity?

◀ *The revolution in Germany in 1918.*

Things to Do

1 Find your local war memorial. Your local newspaper will have records of when it was put up.
2 On what day do we remember the people who died in the First World War? What is the flower that we associate with the war?

Index

aeroplanes, 11, 13, 14, 20
airships, 11, 12, 13, 14, 20
ambulances, 46, 53, 54
army camps, 7, 31, 74
Arras, battle of, 59
Austria, 5, 6, 32, 33

base hospital, 53
beer, 31, 71
Belgium, 5, 6, 8, 9, 36, 37, 40
Böcker, Captain, 13, 14
bombing, 12, 13, 14, 20, 21, 22, 23, 74
Britain, 1, 3, 5, 6, 9, 13, 14, 16, 17, 20, 22, 23, 31, 32, 36, 37, 39, 45, 48, 53, 55, 57, 60, 63, 64, 65, 73, 74
British empire, 1, 73, 74
Brittain, Vera, 2, 24, 42, 43, 53, 54, 70, 83
Buckingham Palace, 6

Carson, Sir Edward, 3
casualty clearing station, 52, 53
Catholics, 3
censorship, 39, 48
Churchill, Winston, 9
civilian, 71
Clark, Andrew, 17, 25, 26, 57, 83
coalition government, 64, 73
Commons, House of, 9, 28
Conscientious objectors, 46
conscription, 26, 57
convalescents, 53, 70
convoy system, 64
courts martial, 28

Defence of the Realm Act, 28, 30, 31
docks, 2, 20, 28
domestic service, 43, 44, 56
drink, 31

enfranchisement, *see vote, right to*
England, 8, 9, 24, 31, 54
Europe, 3, 5, 6, 36, 84

farming, 1, 2, 64, 65
Ferdinand, Archduke Franz, 5, 36
firefighter, 43
first aid post, 51, 52
Folkestone, 20
food, 39, 60, 62, 63, 64, 65, 67, 69, 73

France, 1, 5, 6, 8, 9, 31, 37, 46
Fritz, Captain, 12

Germany, 1, 5, 6, 8, 9, 10, 12, 13, 14, 16, 17, 20, 21, 22, 25, 30, 32, 33, 36, 37, 39, 40, 48, 59, 60, 63, 83, 84
Great Yarmouth, 12, 13
Grey, Lord, 9
guns, 3, 13, 14, 22, 32, 55, 74

Hartlepool, 16
home rule, 3
hospitals, 43, 53, 54, 74, 83
hospital ships, 43
hydrogen, 14

influenza, 83
internment, 60
invasion, 8, 16, 17, 37
Ireland, 1, 3, 6
Italy, 5

Kaiser Wilhelm, 6, 12
Kings Lynn, 13
Kitchener, Lord, 9, 24, 25

Liberal government, 64, 73
Lloyd George, David, 55, 64
London, 8, 13, 33, 40
Lusitania, 33

Macmillan, Crystal, 33
Military Service Act, 45, 73
Ministry of Food, 64, 65
munitions, 44, 55, 56, 57, 71, 73

Netherlands, the, 32
neutral countries, 5, 32
North Sea, 12
Northcliffe, Lord, 48
nurses, 42, 43, 44, 53

Pals Battalions, 24, 25
Pankhurst, Mrs, 4, 30
Parliament, 2, 28, 45
police, 2, 17, 43
prisoners of war (PoWs), 14, 32, 46, 59
Proclamation, Lincolnshire, 17, 18
Protestants, 3
pubs, 31

rationing, 64, 65, 67, 69, 73

recruiting, 24, 25, 26
Red Cross, 42
Royal Army Medical Corps, (RAMC), 52
rumours, 36, 37, 48
Russia, 5, 6, 33, 37

Sarajevo, 5
Sassoon, Siegfried, 21, 22, 70
Scarborough, 16
Scotland, 33, 37, 39
searchlights, 13, 20, 74
Serbia, 5
shells, 16, 55, 57, 58
ships, 1, 7, 11, 16, 20, 39, 64, 69
Somme, battle of, 25, 43, 48, 53, 55
spies, 36
strikes, 2
submarines, 39
suffragettes, 2, 6, 30
suffragists, 2
Sweden, 33

Thompson, Leonard, 1, 59
trade unions, 1, 2, 6
treating, 31
tribunals, 45, 46, 71
Triple Alliance, 5
Triple Entente, 5

unknown soldier, 84
United States of America, (USA), 1, 6, 32, 33, 74
university, 2

Voluntary Aid Detachments, (VADs), 42, 44, 53
vote, right to, 2, 4, 42

Wales, 31
war memorials, 84
Whitby, 16
white feathers, 26
women, 1, 2, 4, 32, 42, 45, 46, 55, 56, 57, 65, 73, 74, 77
women's magazines, 77, 78, 79, 80, 81, 82
Women's Peace Conference, 32, 33
Woolwich Arsenal, 55
wound stripe, 52
Wright Brothers, 11

Zeppelin, Count von, 11
zeppelins, 12, 13, 14, 20, 37, 57, 74